FITNESS WALKING

FITNESS WALKING

LES SNOWDON & MAGGIE HUMPHREYS

MAINSTREAM
PUBLISHING

EDINBURGH AND LONDON

First published in Great Britain 1992 by
MAINSTREAM PUBLISHING COMPANY
(EDINBURGH) LTD
7 Albany Street
Edinburgh EH1 3UG
ISBN 1 85158 482 X (paper)

A catalogue record for this book is available from the British
Library

Book design by WIDE ART, EDINBURGH
Illustrated by IRENE BARRY

Filmset in 11 on 14pt Bembo by
Selwood Systems, Primrose Lane, Midsomer Norton
Printed in Great Britain by Billings & Sons, Worcester

If you are unfit, pregnant or have a diagnosed medical
problem which will affect your ability to exercise, you should
check with your doctor before commencing a vigorous.
fitness walking programme. The authors and publishers
cannot accept responsibility for any injury or damage suffered
as a result of attempting an exercise in this book.

To
G. E. S. and G. W. H.
with love

ON WALKING

It's my life; it's impossible not to walk. It's simply the greatest pleasure.

JOHN HILLABY

Walking . . . blessedness of mere movement, free and careless motion.

JOHN BUCHAN

The difference between a good walker and a bad one is that one walks with his heart, and the other with his feet.

W. H. DAVIES

To all who feel overwhelmed and work weary, the exhilarating exercise of walking offers both a stimulus and a sedative.

ROBERT LOUIS STEVENSON

Man alone, among all living beings, walks erect, because his nature and his being are divine.

ARISTOTLE

If one just keeps on walking everything will be all right.

SOREN KIERKEGAARD

CONTENTS

FOREWORD

Physical inactivity is harmful to health. Physical activity is beneficial to health for all ages and disabilities. Walking is a natural activity and is health promoting, especially in an increasingly sedentary society which is living longer and has more leisure time. Walking is cheap, flexible in time, speed and location to suit any age. Walking is for individuals, families or groups of people.

Les Snowdon and Maggie Humphreys develop a 'walk life-maintenance scheme'. They demonstrate the medical benefits of walking on the cardiovascular system, osteoporosis, stress and obesity, and the benefits of regular walking for relaxation and health.

As a medical practitioner I can thoroughly recommend anyone to read this book and take up the challenge to develop a personal walking programme for life. The medical, physical, psychological and social benefits of regular walking can be demonstrated and a greater independence for living experienced.

Get motivated, start slowly, develop a routine and use this book as a guide for yourself and others.

Fitness walking is fun and beneficial for all. Start the walking habit now – you will soon feel better. Make sure you have the correct footwear. The advice is contained in this readable book. ENJOY IT.

DR DEREK BROWNE MRCP MRCGP MFCH
General Practitioner
Medical Adviser Health Promotion

CHAPTER ONE

WHY WALKING WINS
The Success of
The Walking Diet

All I can give you is the opportunity, the impulse, the key.
HERMANN HESSE

This book is about you!

It's about your fitness, your health, and your happiness.
When you have finished reading it – and you have walked
your way through its pages – you will be fitter and slimmer,
and you will know how to manage your own maintenance
programme that will serve you for the rest of your life.
Because exercise is for life. It's not a short-term cure. You
have to work at it. But the key is to make it fun.

You have a right to be fit. And you have a right to
good health and a long life. But when it comes down to it,
only you can make the changes that will bring you these
benefits. You may have tried and failed with other exercise
routines, but this time you are going to succeed; this time
you are going to be a winner.

But to be a winner you have to accept responsibility
for yourself. Only you are responsible for your heart. Only
you are responsible for your pulse, your blood pressure, your
lungs, your body fat and your cholesterol level. But with a
little help, you will soon learn how to overcome inertia, how
to motivate yourself, how to walk – and how to keep on

walking. This book will give you the opportunity, the impulse and the key. The rest is up to you.

THE WALKING DIET SUCCESS STORY

The Walking Diet was launched in April 1991 and within weeks it was in the bestseller lists throughout Britain and Ireland. After a nationwide publicity tour throughout the United Kingdom, the book had its Irish launch in Dublin on Pat Kenny's late night TV chat show, Kenny Live. A politician, Jim Kemmy, an actress, Eileen Coghan, and two members of the audience, Teresa Corrigan and Julie Stapleton, all volunteered to be weighed and to go away and do The Walking Diet. When the Walking Dieters returned, the ebullient Mr Kenny said: 'After the last show the book walked off the shelves; it was No. 1 in the bestsellers.'

Pat Kenny, a great walker himself, then weighed the dieters, and the results were astonishing. Jim Kemmy, who was very overweight, had lost 42 lb, Julie Stapleton 17 lb, Teresa Corrigan 14 lb, and Eileen Coghan 9 lb.

When Pat Kenny interviewed us initially, and asked us how much weight they could all expect to lose, we had said that a good target was to aim for about 1–2 lb a week. Eileen Coghan had done this easily, but her fellow dieters proved what can be done when you really set your heart on something. Not only did they lose weight, but this is what they all said about walking:

Eileen Coghan: 'I'd recommend it to anybody. I feel as fit as a flea and toned up. I sleep better – like a top – and I have more energy. I loved it, I feel great and I'm going to keep it up.'

Teresa Corrigan: 'The walking was excellent. After a week you felt so good, much fitter with endless energy. You wanted to get up in the mornings and get going.'

Julie Stapleton: 'I loved the walking. I had great energy. After the first week I really enjoyed it.'

And this is what *Jim Kemmy* said after losing his 42 lb on *The Walking Diet*: 'It's a good guide. It gives you the motivation, but it's up to you, basically.'

It's up to you, basically. It is. But with a little help, guidance and motivation from us, you too can join The Walking Dieters above and feel great ... feel fitter ... have endless energy ... be toned up ... sleep like a top ... be dying to get out of bed in the mornings ... and lose – well, that's up to you!

When we wrote *The Walking Diet*, fitness walking as a popular activity was almost unknown in Britain and Ireland. Of course, people had heard of power walking and race walking (the type of walking they do in the Olympics), and walking itself had been growing in popularity for several years. In fact, according to the General Household Survey, walking is now the most popular form of exercise in Britain. And experience seems to confirm this. Wherever we walk, there are increasing numbers of people who are taking to the roads, footpaths, and hills.

But most of the walkers out there are simply walking – they are not engaged in fitness walking. So what is fitness walking?

WALKING AND THE FITNESS REVOLUTION

Fitness walking is at the heart of a revolution which is changing the entire way that people view fitness and health. Since the early 1980s, fitness walking has grown in the USA from an infant activity to being the largest participant fitness activity for people of all ages – and that includes jogging and aerobics.

The figures for sales of sports shoes say it all. Sales of running shoes in the USA have stalled at around $600 million since 1985, but sales of walking shoes have soared from $300 million to $1.5 billion a year over the past five years. It's now official – jogging is passé. Fitness walking is the new kid on the block.

And according to the National Sports Goods Association in the USA, it shows the fastest growth among all fitness activities – up 60 per cent in less than five years, from 41.5 million participants to 66 million. Young children through to adults in their 80s have discovered for themselves the benefits of fitness walking.

Fitness walking is brisk, aerobic walking – a low-impact, low-stress form of exercise. It is not 'power walking', where walkers are pounding the pavements at more than five miles an hour. (This is not a moderate form of exercise; it could just as easily be called 'stress walking'.) And it's not race walking, where walkers pump their arms vigorously backwards and forwards as they stride along at 8–9 miles an hour. It is, however, brisk, aerobic walking which increases the rate at which your heart and lungs work so that you gain all the short- and long-term benefits of aerobic exercise without the risks to your hips, knees and ankles inherent in high-impact work-outs like jogging and aerobics.

14

WHY WALKING WINS

Any type of exercise is better than none, but the best kind of exercise is vigorous, regular aerobic exercise. Aerobic exercise, such as fitness walking, uses the large muscle groups in your legs and arms in a steady rhythmic pattern. As you walk briskly, these muscles need oxygen so you need to breathe more deeply to take it in and your heart needs to pump faster to deliver it.

Fitness walking is more than just walking for fitness – it's walking for total health, and is the cornerstone of a total approach to personal fitness which also includes exercises for improving strength and flexibility, advice on diet, and how to relax and reduce stress.

Fitness walking is changing the way we live, work and exercise. Whichever way you look at it, walking wins every time.

1. FITNESS WALKING – THE BEST EXERCISE

Man has been walking for at least three million years. He has been jogging for 30. The moral is simple: you don't have to break yourself with 'no pain, no gain' jogging – walk, don't run. Fitness walking is a 'best' exercise recommended by exercise physiologists, biomechanical experts, cardiologists, chest experts, obesity experts and stress experts, among others.

Walking has always been a major form of transportation for Man, but only recently have the health and mental benefits of fitness walking become apparent. Today there are over 1,000 walking clubs in the United States alone, plus dozens of exercise physiology labs and programmes studying the beneficial effects of walking.

2. FITNESS WALKING – IT'S EASY, SIMPLE AND SAFE

Fitness walking is suitable for just about everybody. And it's a totally natural activity which can be enjoyed by all the family – from the youngest to the oldest, even those recovering from illness. It can be done almost anywhere, at any time, and it requires no special skills. Using the WALKPLAN and WALKFIT programmes, anyone can soon build up a regular routine which will keep them fit and healthy for the rest of their lives. It can also be done from your front-door. It's not necessary to go anywhere first in order to do it. Just go outside whether you live in the town or country, and enjoy it. If you live in a dense urban area, then find a park or an open space to walk in. And whereas biomechanical studies show that your feet pound the ground with 3–4 times your body weight when jogging, and 4–5 times your body weight when performing dance aerobics, your feet strike the ground with only 1–1.5 times your body weight when fitness walking, making it the safest form of aerobic exercise around.

3. FITNESS WALKING – IT'S INEXPENSIVE

All you need is a pair of comfortable, well-cushioned walking shoes that offer good heel and arch support. No need for expensive designer fashionwear; no need for specialist sports gear; no need for expensive sports club fees. Fitness walking is cheap – so all the family can afford to participate in it.

4. FITNESS WALKING – IT'S AEROBIC

Fitness walking gives you all the aerobic fitness benefits of jogging, cycling, swimming, rowing and dance aerobics – but without the injuries or the 'burn-out'. As a moderate, rhythmic exercise, it is the easiest aerobic exercise of them all. You will find it easy to increase your total oxygen consumption, and therefore your aerobic capacity, and so benefit with long-term fitness and cardiovascular health.

5. FITNESS WALKING – IT MAKES YOU SLIM

Fitness walking will help you get back to your ideal weight and, combined with THE FITNESS WALKER'S DIET, it will help you stay there. When you walk aerobically, your BMR (basal, or resting, metabolic rate) speeds up, and the heart and respiratory rates increase. The increase in oxygen and the increased BMR burn off excess calories and keep them off forever. On average, depending upon weight, you will burn off around 200 calories for every 30 minutes' fitness walking. And walking up an incline or over rough ground can burn off up to 50 per cent more than on an even surface (see Table 1). It is the perfect weight-management system.

6. FITNESS WALKING – THE BEST HIP AND THIGH CONDITIONER

Walking is a perfect massage – it improves both muscle tone and strength. It will tone and strengthen your hips and thighs. And it will do the same for your stomach and buttocks. Combined with THE FITNESS WALKER'S DIET, fitness walking will help you walk away all those flabby areas that you've always wanted to get rid of.

7. FITNESS WALKING – THE BEST WAY TO BEAT STRESS

Fitness walking is a universal stress reliever. It energises you; helps you relax; makes you feel good about yourself; helps you cope with anything that life throws at you, especially in the work place. Walk to work, or part of the way; take a fitness walking break during the day; walk at least part of the way home; or take a walk in the evening. It will help you beat depression, and it will help you sleep better. Fitness walking is the best – and cheapest – stress management system around.

8. FITNESS WALKING – IT'S A POSITIVE ADDICTION

The more walking you do, the more you will want to do. Once fitness walking is a part of your everyday life, you will not want to let a day go by without it. Walking can easily become a lifelong habit and it is the easiest form of exercise to keep up for a lifetime.

As we shall see later, fitness walking can also help with:

* Back pain
* Heart disease
* Bone strength
* Premenstrual syndrome
* Pregnancy
* Hypertension

* Cholesterol
* Respiratory problems
* Cardiac rehabilitation
* Arthritis
* Varicose veins
* Smoking

It is, quite simply, one of the very best forms of exercise available, with benefits which go far beyond the normal expectations of a standard fitness programme.

WALKING SPEED		CALORIES BURNED (APPROX)	
MPH	PACE	IN 30 MIN	IN 1 HOUR
2	SLOW	120	240
2.5	MEDIUM	140	280
3	MEDIUM	160	320
3.5	BRISK	180	360
4	BRISK	210	420
4.5	FAST	250	500
WALKING UP MODERATE INCLINE	BRISK	300	600

TABLE 1

CHAPTER TWO

FITNESS WALKING
The Way Ahead

Whenever I feel the need for taking exercise I go and lie down until the feeling passes away.

GEORGE BERNARD SHAW

I like long walks, especially when they are taken by people who annoy me.

FRED ALLEN

EXERCISE – WHY BOTHER?

A recent report from The British Heart Foundation suggested that lack of exercise can be as bad for us as smoking 20 cigarettes a day, having high blood pressure or high levels of cholesterol. Another independent report indicated that the least active population has almost twice the incidence of heart disease as the most active. In Britain, someone has a heart attack every three minutes, and lack of exercise is a contributory factor. Even in the health-conscious USA, the Public Health Service has estimated that only 20 per cent of American adults take regular exercise, and according to the British Heart Foundation and The Health Education Authority, even fewer than that take enough exercise in this country to benefit their cardiovascular health – that is, exercise which develops a strong heart and blood vessels. Indeed, The Royal College of Physicians recently said that levels of fitness are so low that many Britons are left panting after a brisk walk.

One reason for people taking less exercise, particularly in the West, is that, as the twentieth century has worn on, we have become increasingly sedentary. We spend more time sitting – in houses, offices, cars, buses, trains, planes and so on – and at least half of those people who now buy tennis or running shoes never go running or play tennis. Studies also show that we become even more sedentary as we grow older, and that is bad news not only for our cardiovascular health, but for our general health and fitness.

But we are all more health conscious these days, aren't we? There are more people than ever exercising, going to health clubs, doing aerobics, buying health magazines and videos, than ever before.

Sadly, the statistics speak for themselves: 25 per cent of people taking up fitness programmes today will give them up during the first week. It seems that despite all their best intentions, many people starting out on fitness programmes are destined to fail. Within just one week they are suffering from fitness fatigue.

FITNESS FATIGUE

The fitness business is now big business – £1 billion world-wide. As a result, people are always trying to tell you what the best exercise is. Some say swimming, others jogging, others cycling or rowing, and others favour aerobics in one of its many forms – dance aerobics, step aerobics, water aerobics, and so on. In the '90s gym-speak and fit-speak language, we are being urged to take up funk-aerobics, cardio-funk, body-contouring, cardio-circuits and hydrofitness. And these are only a few of the fitness panaceas on offer to tempt us to spend money and buy fitness products. Trying to decide which fitness routine to follow requires a major decision and only adds to the feeling of fitness fatigue.

Donna Seymour, of the Health Education Authority's *Look After Your Heart* programme, has said: 'We should get away from the idea that fitness equals sport. Fitness equals activity.' We endorse that. To get fit it is not necessary to take part in vigorous sports activities, and no one has to follow some cranky workout programme that bores them out of their mind and leaves them with injured limbs and a sense of failure. Apart from those for whom fitness is a way of life, it seems that many of us find fitness a bit of a bore. At best, we will give it a go – after all, it is good for us. But as for having any fun doing it – forget it!

And that's where we go wrong. Exercise can be fun, and should be fun. According to Professor Morris of the Health Education Authority, 'Exercise is today's best buy in Public Health; for the individual there can't be many better ways of spending one or two per cent of his or her time.'

When you are fit and healthy you are in control of your life. Your body is supple and you have reserves of strength and stamina. Suppleness prevents you getting injured and helps keep you active as you get older. Increased strength helps you get around, carry loads and climb upstairs. And stamina keeps you going through the day without getting tired. Exercise is the best investment you can make for a long, healthy life. But it should meet our individual needs, be safe and effective, and everyone should be able to do it, regardless of the state of fitness that they start out from. And there's only one form of exercise that offers all this – fitness walking.

Fitness walking four times a week, for 30 minutes at a time at a moderately brisk rate, will build cardiovascular and respiratory fitness and, according to the Aerobics Institute in the USA, provide all the fitness benefits normally associated with the 'no pain, no gain' formula, as well as providing protection against cardiovascular disease, cancers and a wide range of other health problems. Together with ten minutes of stretching exercises a few times a week, you will have a total fitness programme that you can work happily with for the rest of your life. And above all – it's fun to do.

Other popular exercises all have their drawbacks. For swimming to be effective as a cardiovascular exercise, it is necessary to swim for 30 minutes three times a week: how many people have the time to get to a swimming-pool to do this? And there aren't even enough swimming pools to go round. Recent studies show that there is only scope for 1 or 2 per cent of the population to have daily exercise through swimming. Cycling is a good form of exercise, too, but needs to be done at sufficient intensity and several times a week for it to be effective. And it can be dangerous: 9,000 cyclists are injured on British roads every year. Aerobic dance and movement are popular forms of exercise as well, but studies published in *The Physician* and *Sportsmedicine* found that, according to the 76 per cent of the aerobics instructors who responded to a questionnaire, 43 per cent of the people attending their classes sustained injuries from the activity. Feet, ankle, shin, calf, knee and lower back problems were common. And rowing is also popular with some people, but is not practical as an exercise for everyone to do. And rowing machines, like exercise bicycles and skipping, have a low boredom threshold.

And then there's jogging.

WHAT'S WRONG WITH JOGGING?

On 20 July 1984, Jim Fixx, at 52 years old, the arch guru of jogging and author of the bestselling book, *The Complete Book of Running*, left his motel in the small Vermont town of Hardwick, USA, and began a jog which was to be the last of his life. An hour later, his mud-stained body was discovered by a grassy verge on a country road, little more than 30 yards from his motel. The news of his death stunned America. How could Jim Fixx, the ultimate exercise guru, die in this way?

Fixx was a one-time magazine editor who had become a bestselling author. Yet in spite of his success, he had not found happiness. He had changed jobs several times and been through a divorce. And he found the pressures of public life and continual interviews a strain.

Jim Fixx became a runner in his late 30s. Before then, he had habitually eaten high-fat foods, had an extremely high cholesterol level, and was considerably overweight. He had been a heavy smoker for many years and there was a history of heart disease in his family. After several years of running ten miles a day, Jim Fixx might well have been fit, but he was not healthy.

Although he had escaped the high-pressure world of advertising, he had substituted this with a high-pressure lifestyle. He had used jogging to break away from stress, but ironically, jogging had broken him.

Although jogging did not cause Fixx's death, his death did lead people to understand that this form of exercise is not the only way to lead a healthy life. Since 1984, increasing numbers of people of all ages in America have stopped jogging. Instead, they have discovered that fitness walking is a much more realistic approach to lifelong health and fitness. Of those who still start jogging programmes, statistics show that around

60 per cent drop out or burn out within three months. In contrast, the drop-out rate for walking programmes is less than 25 per cent.

The message is simple: walk, don't run.

FITNESS WALKING AND HEALTH

By health I mean the power to live a full, adult, living, breathing life in close contact with what I love – I want to be all that I am capable of being.

KATHERINE MANSFIELD

The World Health Organization defines a healthy body as one that is in a 'state of complete physical and mental well-being'. Health is a holistic concept; it involves caring for yourself and developing your body and inner resources to the full so that you can get the most out of life. It is a state of total well-being and optimum functioning with the absence of disease.

When we are healthy we can meet any challenge and cope with the stresses and strains of life. Fitness, on the other hand, only allows you to perform work more efficiently and with less effort. And as we discovered with Jim Fixx, you can be fit without being healthy.

Fitness walking is not only about fitness; it is also about health. An effective programme aimed at optimum health should include moderate exercise (fitness walking), a balanced, nutritious diet (see THE FITNESS WALKER'S DIET), adequate sleep, and keeping your body weight within its ideal limits for your height and frame. Stress needs to be managed effectively, alcohol should be consumed only in moderation, and smoking should be cut out altogether.

Exercise on its own cannot help you attain optimum

health. But exercise can help you accomplish it; and the easiest way to develop optimum health is to do regular fitness walking and follow THE FITNESS WALKER'S DIET. You will look better, feel better, sleep better and have endless energy. You won't need to take tranquillisers. You won't want to smoke. And your self-confidence and self-esteem will grow. You will be in balance – fit, healthy and whole.

WALKING – THE BEST EXERCISE

Walking makes for a long life.

HINDU PROVERB

For several million years, Man has been walking with an upright gait. For several thousand years, walking has been used as a means of travel and has been valued for its contribution to health and longevity. Aristotle, the Greek philosopher, wrote: 'Man alone, among all living beings walks erect, because his nature and his being are divine.'

In the twentieth century, studies with infants have shown that from around one year old, when the child makes its first attempt to walk, an upright gait and movement are part of the development of cerebral function – the ability to know and reason. Pieper, an expert on the development of cerebral function, has remarked: 'Progress is made possible by the strong urge for movement and activity, which continuously drives the child to new experiments.' Our bodies are built for action and movement. The mechanics of walking are as much a part of the human body as the mechanics of respiration and heart function. And as a way of getting from one place to another, the body reaches its highest state of physical perfection in the act of walking.

For over 40 years now, studies have shown walking

to be the best exercise that people of all ages can do. In the 1950s, two studies linked walking to a decreased risk of heart disease. The first was with London bus drivers who got very little exercise; they were compared with bus conductors who walked up and down the bus aisles collecting fares. In another study, in the USA, sedentary postal clerks were compared to postmen who walked daily to deliver mail. In both studies the walkers had fewer heart attacks.

A study of executive grade civil servant office workers found that those who took part in vigorous exercise in their leisure time developed less than half the amount of heart disease of their colleagues who took no exercise. Another study carried out among sedentary women aged 42 who undertook a modest programme of sustained brisk walking recorded changes in their blood which protected them against coronary heart disease. Indeed, a recent report from the Royal College of Physicians said that even couch potatoes can improve their health in a few weeks if they start walking regularly. The first four-minute miler, Sir Roger Bannister, who helped to compile it, said: 'Activity has largely disappeared from work and has to be introduced through a change of lifestyle.' And the Health Education Authority has this to say about the value of walking: 'The dynamic exercise from walking is an excellent stamina-building activity.'

But one of the most comprehensive series of studies ever carried out on exercise and health was The College Alumni Study by Dr Ralph Paffenberger and his associates at Stanford University in the USA. The studies followed the health habits of 17,000 Harvard graduates for over 20 years, and found that those who exercised regularly were significantly less likely to suffer or die from heart attacks than their less active colleagues. And it was walking that was the most popular exercise reported.

The study found that men who walked nine or more miles a week had a 21 per cent lower mortality rate than those who walked three miles or less, and that moderate exercise such as walking could add up to two years to a person's life.

FITNESS WALKING – THE EXERCISE OF THE '90s

Although walking as a moderate exercise has been proved to reduce health risks and prolong life, it is the aerobic benefits of 'fitness walking' which really provide the long-term health benefits. The idea of aerobic exercise – aerobic means 'with oxygen' – has been popular since the 1960s when Dr Kenneth Cooper wrote the bestselling book *Aerobics* and started a worldwide aerobics fitness craze.

Since oxygen cannot be stored in the body, and our cells need continuous amounts of it to maintain health, aerobic exercise increases our normal capacity to process oxygen; this results in an improved cardiovascular and respiratory system. Walking aerobically causes the body to take in more air with less effort. The lungs are then able to extract more oxygen from the increased air supply and deliver it to the cells where it is needed to combine with food to produce energy.

The result is an improvement in the vital efficiency of the lungs and the whole cardiovascular system. Not only does it pump blood more efficiently, but the total volume of blood actually increases. The heart becomes bigger and stronger, and the blood vessels enlarge and become more elastic. Blood flow to the muscles is improved; muscles and ligaments are strengthened; joints become more mobile and stronger.

One of the main ways to determine fitness – cardiovascular fitness – is to measure the consumption and utilisation of oxygen, O_2. The maximum rate at which you consume oxygen depends on the capacity and efficiency of the cardiovascular system, and this is normally expressed by the abbreviation VO_2max. It is the goal of aerobic exercise to condition the body and increase VO_2max.

Anaerobic ('without air') exercise, in contrast to aerobic exercise, generates energy without oxygen. Whereas regular, continuous aerobic exercise provides a greater volume of oxygen and makes the body more efficient, anaerobic exercise, such as squash (a stop-start activity requiring short, sudden bursts of energy), places heavy demands on the body for oxygen – and puts the body into 'oxygen debt'. When this happens, lactic acid is formed as a waste product, causing muscle fatigue, soreness and sometimes pain. Rapid heart beat and breathlessness are also typical effects of anaerobic exercise.

Since the 1960s, the benefits of aerobic exercise have been widely researched and medical authorities now recommend that aerobic exercise performed for a minimum of 20–30 minutes, three to four times a week at what is known as your 'training heart rate' (see YOUR TARGET HEART RATE in Chapter Four – WALKFIT), will give you a good cardiovascular workout, and provide lifelong protection against disease.

The Health Education Authority, the British Medical Association and The American College of Sports Medicine all recommend moderate activity such as fitness walking to provide beneficial aerobic exercise. BUPA (British United Provident Association), the health insurance company, in advice it gives about training programmes, says: 'Aerobic exercise is one of the keys to improving and maintaining fitness and well-being.' And they recommend walking as a

29

safe way of fitness training. And studies carried out in the Exercise Physiology and Nutrition Laboratory at the University of Massachusetts Medical School in the 1980s concluded that fitness walking raised the heart rate to an appropriate level in 90 per cent of individuals, irrespective of age or physical condition.

However, the area where fitness walking really scores is in long-term health benefits. Short-term fitness goals are not enough. All the research done over the past 25 years on the relationship between exercise and health has concluded that the main health benefits only come when exercise is consistent and lifelong. If exercise is not kept up, the body very quickly reverts to its inactive state. It can take three to six months of regular aerobic exercise to build up a strong heart and powerful lungs; and it can take the same period of inactivity to lose it all.

Fitness walking is the exercise most recommended to achieve these long-term aims. It is easy to do and is easy to keep up because it is a continuous rhythmic activity which soon becomes habit-forming.

We hope you are now totally convinced that fitness walking will provide all the aerobic benefits of other more extreme forms of exercise, and that you are ready to get started on the journey of a lifetime to fitness, health and happiness. But if it's all as easy as this, why are so many of us still not trying it?

Well – much of the evidence for the benefits of fitness walking has only become available in the past ten years, and it takes time for new knowledge to become widely available. And then, of course, there are all the usual excuses that everyone uses to get away from having to exercise.

EXCUSES, EXCUSES

Exercise! — that sounds like hard work to me.

It seems that many people do think that exercise is too much like hard work. They may even think of it as an X-rated activity — Xercise! — something best to be avoided. This is true for many people who start out on strenuous exercise programmes, injure themselves and give it all up; but if you start out with a moderate programme like brisk fitness walking and build up gradually, then you will enjoy it and you won't want to give it up.

Exercise! — I haven't got the time. I'm too busy.

Just 20 to 30 minutes fitness walking three to four times a week will give you all the long-term fitness and cardiovascular benefits that you need, and will help to keep you slim. Once you start to feel the benefits, and walking becomes a regular habit, you will want to find the time to get out. Try getting up earlier on a morning to walk; walk during lunchtimes; walk in your work breaks instead of drinking coffee or smoking; walk in the evening instead of settling down in a chair in front of the television.

Exercise! — I need relaxation, not exercise.

Fitness walking is one of the best forms of relaxation around. It relieves stress by helping you to get away from telephones and all the noise and distractions of life, and it helps you to take your mind off your problems and to rediscover an inner peace. After a session of brisk fitness walking you will feel calm and relaxed and you will want to find time regularly to get out and recapture this feeling. Indeed, studies have shown that exercise such as this can lift depression and help you sleep better.

31

Exercise! – I'd be too embarrassed.

We have all seen the ardent jogger pounding his way along the pavements, puffing and panting as though his life depended on it; and we have all seen the new jogger out with a shiny new shell-suit and training shoes – and we've thought 'rather you than me'. So why not try fitness walking? All you need is a pair of comfortable walking shoes and off you go. There's no need to be embarrassed – you are going to be walking a little faster than other people, but you will look and feel better doing it. And, in the stakes for fitness and health, you will be leaving them far behind. Remember: fitness walking is not a sport – it's an enjoyable exercise.

Exercise! – I'm too old for it.

You are never too old to start exercising. Provided you take into account any diagnosed medical problems and consult with your doctor first, then you can start out on a programme of fitness walking and build up gradually to an aerobic conditioning programme that will benefit you for the rest of your life.

Exercise! – I'm too fat. I'd rather diet.

You may not realise it, but you will benefit more from a regular programme of exercise like fitness walking, together with a low-fat high-fibre nutritious diet, than you will from dieting alone. Fitness walking will help you slim and stay slim by burning up the calories. If you burn more calories than you eat, your body will begin to use its own energy stores and fat will start to disappear.

Exercise! – That sounds boring.

It's not that we don't try to exercise – we do. We just give up too soon because we often forget that there are ways to make exercise fun. Studies show that one out of every two people who start an exercise programme drop out within the first six months and half of those quit during the first week. This is where fitness walking scores. Fitness walking is fun. After a short time, you will feel great, have increased energy, improved concentration and a heightened sense of well-being. When it comes to fun, fitness walking scores every time.

In the next chapter, the WALKPLAN will get you started on the road to fitness walking. We hope that it will set you going on the journey of a lifetime, and that from now on you will never look back. One expert has estimated that, for every hour of fitness walking, you can add one extra hour to the length of your life. So get started now. Fitness, health, happiness and a long life are within your grasp.

CHAPTER THREE

WALKPLAN
Your Personal Conditioning Programme

The journey of a thousand miles begins with just one step.

LAO TSE

DON'T JUST SIT THERE – START WALKING!

You made the first step towards that new, exciting, slim, fit and healthy you when you decided to learn more about fitness walking. You may have tried and failed with other fitness programmes, but this time it's for real. This time you are in charge. This time you are going to succeed.

You may not have realised it, but you are already an accomplished walker. Yes – it's true. If you think about it, you began to walk when you were around one year old – when you were able to stand up, balance yourself and take the first step towards your future independence. You were no longer stuck on all fours; you gained the use of your legs. And that was a great leap forwards.

Since then you have been taking on average 10,500 steps (equivalent to four miles) each day, amounting to nearly four million steps (1,500 miles) each and every year.

Your face is already lighting up. You are thinking to yourself, 'Things can't be so bad if I do all that walking.' But the problem is that the four miles you do walk are made up of all the accumulated steps you take during the day, from the moment you get up, to the moment you go to bed: walking around the house, walking outdoors, walking around your workplace. And all this walking is not enough to develop cardiovascular fitness. It is not the amount of walking that you do, but the way that you walk that matters.

Believe it or not, even though you are walking those four miles each day, many of you will still be sedentary. Put simply, that means that you will be spending too much time sitting and not enough time exercising – too much time sitting at desks all day at work, sitting in cars, buses and trains, and sitting in chairs at home watching TV. In Britain alone it is now estimated that the average person watches up to 24 hours of TV a week. Hardly surprising then that so many people have heart attacks so young. The rot sets in early.

The British Heart Foundation and the Aerobics Institute in America both advise that to develop long-term fitness means developing cardiovascular fitness – that is, not only strengthening your system against cardiovascular disease but also against death from a wide range of other causes. And as we have seen, to achieve this level of cardiovascular fitness it is necessary to do some aerobic exercise such as fitness walking for a minimum of 20–30 minutes three to four times a week.

Now, this is not too difficult for you. After all, you are already an accomplished walker. All you need now is motivation and a plan to work to, and you will soon be chalking up the necessary number of miles each week to develop long-term health and fitness. But first, some advice for those of you who are out of condition.

HEALTH ADVICE – Read this before proceeding any further

Not everyone should plunge straight into vigorous fitness walking without a gradual build-up to it. If you are uncertain about your physical condition, if you are overweight, suffer from cardiovascular or respiratory disease, have a medically diagnosed problem, or are pregnant, then you should consult your doctor before starting to walk briskly.

And don't let passive fitness deceive you. Just because you are thin and have never suffered a day's illness in your life doesn't mean that you can embark on a vigorous walking programme without building up to it. Don't try and push too hard too quick. Your body is not built to cope with that level of stress. You are starting out on a walking programme to beat stress, not to add to it.

As we get older our bodies respond differently. They are less flexible and they heal more slowly, taking longer to recover from workouts. And increasing years bring with them a loss of muscle power and therefore strength. According to Hal Higdon, a fitness writer, after the age of 30, muscle fibre declines at 3–5 per cent each decade. This can add up to a decline in muscle power of about 30 per cent by the age of 60.

That's the bad news; now for the good news. Fitness walking will help you regain some of that lost muscle strength as well as improve your cardiovascular and respiratory efficiency, although you will still need to exercise the upper body by doing some additional exercises for strength and flexibility. This is why the concept of 'total fitness' is so important: you use fitness walking as your main aerobic conditioner and supplement it with simple stretching exercises for total body fitness.

YOU PUT YOUR RIGHT FOOT FORWARDS

You have already taken the first step back to fitness when you decided to put out of your mind all those failed exercise attempts and give fitness walking a chance.

It was L. P. Hartley who wrote: 'The past is a foreign country; they do things differently there.' Forget about the past. Forget about all the times you tried to get a regular exercise routine going using jogging, cycling, swimming or some other form of workout. All these attempts are behind you; you did things differently then. Now you know that you are an accomplished walker; now you are more motivated; now you are going to succeed.

The next seven steps will help to motivate you and get you started.

1. CHOOSE YOUR WALKING SHOES

Walking is the cheapest form of exercise to do. This is one reason why it has become so popular – it's absolutely free. You need no expensive equipment, no special clothing; there are no membership fees to think about and no coaching fees or travel costs to pay. The only essential item is – a pair of comfortable walking shoes.

2. START SLOWLY

If you have been sedentary for some time and are generally unfit, then you will need to start slowly and ease yourself into a regular exercise programme, beginning with WALKPLAN, your own personal conditioning programme later in this chapter.

This will start you walking at a comfortable pace, and will gradually allow you to build up the time you spend walking each day. That's all you will be thinking about at this stage – the amount of *time* you put in each day. Stopwatches and pedometers are best avoided because they can easily discourage you or cause you to push yourself too hard too soon.

3.   WATCH YOUR WEIGHT

You will feel better and exercise better if you are at your ideal body weight. Since fitness walking is the easiest aerobic exercise for most people to do, it is the easiest way to lose weight and keep slim. By combining a well-balanced nutritious diet with regular fitness walking, you can easily get back to and maintain your ideal weight. THE FITNESS WALKER'S DIET in Chapter 6 will show you how to do this.

4.   WALK WITH OTHERS

You may find it easy to start out on a fitness walking programme alone; you may even prefer it. But if you find it difficult to get motivated, then ask a friend along, take your spouse, take the kids, or get a group together. Group support is often one of the best ways to keep a routine up and achieve results. Think of all the ways you could do this. You might want to organise a fitness walking group at work and get out during the lunch-hour or after work.

5.   START A WALKING DIARY

Keeping a record of when and where you plan to walk will help to keep you motivated – apart from a good pair of walking shoes it's the best investment you can make. It will help you to form a clear idea of your goals and objectives.

Research has shown that people who work towards well-defined goals achieve more than those who simply muddle on from day to day with no clear aims in mind. Self-confidence is boosted when you realise that you can achieve the goals which you set for yourself.

The entries you make in your diary need only be brief and will take little time to fill in. Your walking diary should be a pleasure to fill in, not a chore, and can be used together with the fitness walking programmes that follow later in the book.

6.   KEEP IT UP

Fitness is for life; there are no short-term cures. When you start out on your fitness walking programme you will be full of enthusiasm and you will want to achieve results as quickly as possible. But there may come a time when your initial enthusiasm begins to wane and you approach the danger-point where you are tempted to break your routine. The problem here is that small improvements in aerobic fitness can very quickly disappear. Two weeks of fitness walking will get you started on the road to aerobic fitness, but a two-week period of inactivity will lose any gains you may have made. When you have been walking regularly for a few months, however, your aerobic fitness will be little affected by short lay-offs, but until then you need to stick with the four-week fitness walking programme and the maintenance programme in the next chapter.

7.   ACCEPT SORE MUSCLES

During the period when you first start walking it is easy to strain yourself. If you do, though, don't stop walking entirely.

Slow down a little, listen to your body and keep walking regularly until you are ready to increase the pace again.

Some soreness is inevitable if you are out of condition or have not exercised for years. If you feel stiff or have sore muscles after a workout, then rest between sessions. And when you start out again, always remember to do some stretching exercises to limber up the body first (see Chapter 5), letting your body tell you when you can increase the pace and duration of the workout.

Over the next two weeks you will be starting out with a programme of moderate fitness walking which will tone and condition your body in preparation for the four-week WALKFIT programme in the next chapter.

WALKPLAN is designed to cater for people of all ages and levels of fitness. If your normal lifestyle is sedentary, it will take a couple of weeks for you to build up the stamina required for the four-week fitness walking programme ahead. If you are already fit as a result of doing other exercise, then you will quickly be able to work your way through this section or, indeed, move straight on to WALKFIT itself in Chapter 4.

WALKPLAN – YOUR PERSONAL CONDITIONING PROGRAMME

If you can't talk while you walk – you're going too fast!

If you have never done any aerobic exercise before, or you are not used to walking regularly, then this is where to start. This programme is designed to ease you gently into walking and to prepare you for the aerobic exertion required in the four-week fitness walking programme which follows.

And ease is what it's all about. You're not going to throw yourself into a vigorous workout programme in an all-or-nothing fling. You may have tried this type of approach before and failed; and it's often the reason why so many people give up exercise programmes – we have already seen that surveys show that 25 per cent of people who start an exercise programme quit during the first week. But this is not going to happen to you, is it?

The reason why walking is so effective as an exercise and why it is so easy to keep up is that you are starting out as a fully competent professional. After all, you have been walking since you were about a year old. All you are doing now is setting out to regain some of the body suppleness and stamina that you have lost. So you have to treat your body gently, treat your muscles gently, and ease your way back into an exercise and fitness routine that you can stick with for the rest of your life.

Walking moderately for four days each week, you are gradually going to build up so that after two weeks you can comfortably walk for 20 minutes without becoming tired and without getting injured. You are not going to concern yourself with distance, speed or target heart rates; you are only going to concern yourself with the amount of time that you walk.

Days 1–7

The easiest way to get into a regular walking habit is to walk close to your home. If you have to get somewhere before you walk – the park, the beach, the hills – then there is always room for excuses to get in the way and prevent you starting. Make it easy for yourself by planning out a circular route from your front door around the block and back again, lasting for a minimum of 20 minutes. If it's not easy to do this, then pick

WALKPLAN

	Pace	Time Planned (Mins)	Time Walked (Mins)	Comments
Day 1	Moderate	10		
Day 3	Moderate	10–15		
Day 5	Moderate	10–15		
Day 7	Moderate	15		
	Weekly total			

TABLE 2

the closest convenient point to your home and begin from there.

On Days 1 to 7, your plan is to walk on alternate days for a minimum of ten minutes and a maximum of 15 minutes. This plan is personal to you, so you will decide what feels comfortable and what you can achieve without getting out of breath and feeling fatigued. If you can't talk while you walk, then you're going too fast; slow down to a pace that is more comfortable.

Some of you will be using muscles that you haven't used for years, so you need to push yourself gently a little more each time you get out, walking a little further each time. Remember that all you are doing is limbering up. You are like a professional athlete who is out of condition; you need to get back into training. If ten minutes seems quite enough to begin with, then stick at that until you feel comfortable increasing the time to 12 or 15 minutes.

The WALKPLAN is designed for those people who are able to increase their walking time gently over a two-week period from ten to 20 minutes. But for those of you who still find this too strenuous, then use the plan for as many weeks as you need until you are able to walk comfortably and regularly for 20 minutes at a moderate pace. You may wish to photocopy the WALKPLAN in order to use it several times.

Filling in the WALKPLAN is a help to motivation, so each time you walk you should enter the actual time you walked for and make any comments you wish about the route, the terrain or the weather. Now is also a good time to start your walking diary in which you might want to record more detailed information about your walks and any personal information along the way. You might want to record how you felt and any special thoughts you had, and so on. In the

INNER WALKING chapter later in the book we will be talking about how you can get more out of your walking than simply fitness.

More important, though, the WALKPLAN and your walking diary will help you to maintain the regularity and consistency that you need to make your training programme a success. And it will help to make your walking more fun.

Days 9–15

Walking on alternate days, continue at a moderate pace, but increase the time you spend exercising so that you are now walking for between 15 and 20 minutes each day, gradually building up your time as the week goes by. By the end of this week, you should be able to walk comfortably for 20 minutes without tiring, and be ready to start on the 20 minutes a day required by the WALKFIT programme in the next chapter.

As with the first week of the WALKPLAN, if at any time you feel that the plan is too strenuous, then go back and keep walking at a pace that is comfortable until you are ready to move on to the next level. This is your own personal conditioning programme, so walk to suit your physical condition and listen to what your body is telling you. Table 4 is a blank version of the WALKPLAN. Copy it if you wish, and use it as many times as you need to in order to achieve the required 20 minutes a day.

WALKPLAN

	Pace	Time Planned (Mins)	Time Walked (Mins)	Comments
Day 9	Moderate	15		
Day 11	Moderate	15–20		
Day 13	Moderate	15–20		
Day 15	Moderate	20		
Weekly total				

TABLE 3

WALKPLAN

Day	Pace	Time Planned (Mins)	Time Walked (Mins)	Comments
	Moderate			
	Moderate			
	Moderate			
	Moderate			
	Weekly total			

TABLE 4

CHAPTER FOUR

WALKFIT
Your Four-Week Fitness Walking Programme

I travel not to go anywhere, but to go.
ROBERT LOUIS STEVENSON

If you have completed the WALKPLAN conditioning programme then you have literally taken the first steps towards being a fitness walker. You have proved to yourself that you can keep motivated and stretch yourself a little further each time you walk. You have begun to build the stamina and suppleness needed to keep up a regular exercise programme. And you have begun to rediscover the joy and magic of walking.

Not only are you regaining lost fitness and health, but you are regaining your senses. At 3–4 miles an hour the world looks and feels a different place. Outside on the road you see things differently and your perception affects your whole being – body and mind. You will feel better, more relaxed, more confident.

Rather than being a time in which you have to force yourself to exercise, you won't be able to hold yourself back. Away from the incessant noise of indoor activity, you will have regained a sense of personal space. Your 'walking time' will be the best part of the day – a precious time that you can't wait to repeat.

Although you have been walking moderately until

now, you will already have improved your aerobic capacity and will be ready for the real aerobic benefits provided by fitness walking. And you will know the feeling of exhilaration that you get when you set foot outside each time and breathe in life-giving oxygen.

You will know what it feels like to walk on air.

GETTING STARTED

This is where to begin your programme of aerobic fitness walking. Those of you who are already fit or have done regular aerobic exercise before may have skipped the WALK-PLAN and be starting here.

Getting the most out of fitness walking means 'having a good workout'. And that means that it should:

* meet your individual needs
* be safe and effective
* gradually increase your aerobic capacity
* improve your cardiovascular and respiratory efficiency
* burn away fat and unwanted calories
* keep you motivated.

In other words, if fitness walking is to meet your individual needs and be safe and effective, then you should walk to suit your physical condition. And this applies particularly to anyone who has been sedentary for some time, or who is unsure of their physical condition.

WALK TO SUIT YOUR PHYSICAL CONDITION

Your resting pulse rate is a rough guide to your general physical condition. Acting like a barometer, it is a measure of your state of well-being, stress or illness. To get an accurate measurement it should be taken first thing in the morning before it has had time to be increased by exertion, mental excitement, eating, or stimulants like tea, coffee or nicotine. Taking your pulse rate is quite easy. You can use either of the following two methods:

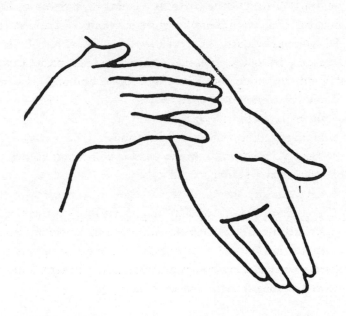

FIG. 1 RADIAL PULSE CAN BE FELT IN THE WRIST.
Turn the palm of the hand towards the ceiling and lightly place three fingers of the other hand on the bare wrist just above the heel of the thumb.

. Your pulse rate varies throughout the day. At its lowest whilst sleeping, it rises from five to ten beats a minute when you awake, and during the day it will rise gradually and can be up to ten beats higher at bedtime than it was when you got up in the morning.

Under normal circumstances, the lower the resting pulse rate, the healthier you are. The average for men is between 70 and 85 a minute; a woman's pulse tends to be faster at 75–90 beats a minute. Most people who have a resting pulse rate between 90 and 100 tend to be unfit, but it is dangerous to generalise. Some people have normal pulse rates up to 100 and some athletes have pulse rates as low as 40. If you are concerned about yours, then you should see a doctor before continuing with a vigorous programme of fitness walking.

One thing we do know is that if you are unfit, then a regular routine of fitness walking will steadily lower the resting pulse rate and this is good news for your long-term health and fitness. The heart is a pump. The less work it has to do throughout your life – the less beats it has to make – the longer it will last.

Walking is safe and effective because it is a low-impact exercise and it uses muscles which you have been using all your life. Even so, when you start out to walk for aerobic fitness it is still necessary to prepare your body – and particularly certain muscles – for the exertion ahead. You need to warm up first.

YOUR WALKFIT WARM-UP

Your body is like a car. Imagine how a car would perform if you accelerated away quickly from a cold start. It would

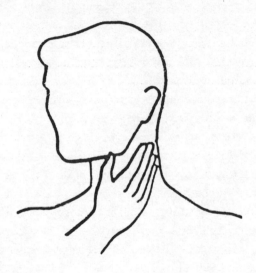

FIG. 2 CAROTID PULSE

This can be felt in the neck just below the ear lobe and forwards toward
the adam's apple. Feel with the fingers – do not press too hard and on
one side of the neck only. (The carotid artery supplies the brain!)
If you press too hard the blood flow is stopped and no pulsations will
be felt. The pulse rate (heart rate) is usually expressed in terms of beats
per minute. So, count the number of pulsations (beats) in 15 seconds and
multiply by four. For example: 17 beats in 15 seconds

$17 \times 4 = 68$ beats per minute

Remember to start your count with zero.

51

cough.and splutter and let you know that it was unhappy with the way you were driving it. Your body is the same and, like a car, it needs warming up first.

There are good physiological reasons why you should warm up before you do vigorous aerobic exercise (this also applies to cooling down which we will discuss later). Warming up is a useful way to check on how your body feels – and it's taking note of how your body feels that makes fitness walking such an easy and effective exercise. Simply listen to what your body is telling you: if it tells you that you are pushing too hard, too fast, then ease off a bit until you feel comfortable again. You should be loosening up the muscles, not straining. Your body always tells the truth – your body is always right.

This advice applies as much to warming up as it does to fitness walking itself. Many people don't take the time to get ready for exercise. They go full out to get results and get injured in the process, giving up before they've started and joining the ever-growing numbers who start and fail with exercise programmes.

Warming up first helps prevent injuries. Blood flow increases to the muscles, and surrounding connective tissue is loosened, so reducing the risk of pulls and tears to muscles, tendons, ligaments and other connective tissue. And increased muscle temperature improves mechanical efficiency: you can walk faster with less effort.

Warm-ups help relieve stiff, tight muscles and they can help reduce the workload on your heart by putting it under less strain all at once. And warm-ups also provide you with psychological benefits. They help you to prepare mentally for the walk ahead and provide a point of focus for you to concentrate on.

Begin your warm-up with brisk walking on the spot, bringing your knees up high so that your thighs are parallel with the ground and swinging your arms back and forth. Doing this for a few minutes will get your circulation moving. Then continue with the warm-up routine illustrated below.

The warm-up routine should not take long, and should always be done before brisk fitness walking. It helps improve circulation and suppleness, and it relaxes the large muscle group on the front of the thigh (the quadriceps), the hamstring muscles at the back of the thigh, and the back of the calves and the achilles tendons, all of which play an important part in fitness walking. Muscles work much better when relaxed, and it is easier to find your stride and get into a good walking rhythm.

1. REACH FOR THE SKY
To increase circulation and activate and limber muscles

Stand with feet hip-width apart. Breathing in, bring hands up over your head so that you feel a mild stretching sensation lifting you upwards from your abdomen. Hold for the count of 5 and relax. Repeat 5 times.

2. SIDE STRETCH

To stretch out the waist, back and sides and loosen the lower spine

Stand with feet hip-width apart. Raise both hands above head and clasp left wrist with right hand. Gently pull wrist to right side, stretching upwards and slightly over from the waist. Hold for 10 seconds. Repeat 5 times. Repeat on other side.

3. SHOULDER CIRCLES

To loosen and relax the neck, shoulders and back

Stand, arms at sides, with feet shoulder-width apart. Gently lift shoulders and move them backwards in a continuous rolling motion. Repeat 5 times, then repeat with a forward rolling motion.

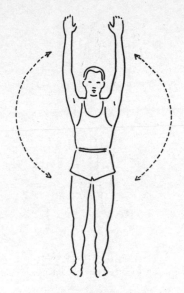

4. ARM CIRCLING
To mobilise the shoulders and chest

Circle both arms, reaching up above head, then out and down to complete
circle. Breathe in as arms lift, out as they come down. Repeat 5 times.

5. CALF RAISES
To strengthen the feet, ankles and calves

Stand with feet together, arms stretched out in front. (For balance, you
might need to support yourself by resting your hands on the back of a
chair.) Lift up on to the balls of the feet. Hold for 5 seconds, then lower.
Repeat 5 times.

6. ACHILLES STRETCH
To stretch out the calves

Stand with your left foot forward. Bend it gently, keeping the right leg straight, heel on the ground. Both feet should be pointing forwards and you should support yourself by resting both hands on your left thigh. Hold for 10 seconds and repeat on the other side.

7. THIGH STRETCH
To stretch out the quadriceps down the front of the thigh

Stand on left leg, clasping right foot with left hand and using a chair for balance. Gently pull foot up, stretching the front of the right thigh. Keep your pelvis tucked forwards and knees close together. Hold for 15 seconds. Repeat on other side.

8. HALF SQUATS
To strengthen the thighs

With feet hip-width apart, and holding on to the back of a chair for
support, squat down, making sure that the angle at the knee is never less
than 90 degrees. Keep your upper body upright. Return to the starting
position. Repeat 10 times.

9. LYING HAMSTRING STRETCH
To improve suppleness

Lie on floor with knees bent and feet flat against ground. Draw right knee
in towards chest, making sure you don't arch your back, and clasp with
both hands just above knee. Slowly straighten leg until you feel a gentle
stretch. Hold for 10–20 seconds. Repeat on other side.

10. KNEE CLASP
To release tension in stomach and back

Lie with back flat on floor, legs together outstretched. Breathing deeply from abdomen, pull knees towards chest one by one. Breathe out, clasping knees and pressing lower back down. Hold for 10 seconds.

WALK YOUR WAY TO HEALTH AND FITNESS

Once you have done several minutes of stretching exercises, the best way to continue warming up is to walk. Your four-week walking programme will now introduce you to the real benefits of aerobic fitness walking after which you will be able to stride out whenever you wish and walk your way to fitness and health.

You can walk anywhere that is convenient and safe, but one of the easiest ways, as you will have already discovered through the WALKPLAN, is to walk out of your own front door and do a circuit, or a number of circuits, around the block and back again. This makes fitness walking a door-to-door personal exercise and it is the easiest and quickest way to keep yourself motivated.

If you have finished the WALKPLAN in the last chapter, or you are already fit and are starting with this programme, then you should be able to walk for a minimum of 20 minutes at a moderate pace without getting out of breath or becoming fatigued.

For the first three weeks, the WALKFIT programme alternates brisk fitness walking with moderate walking for four days a week, then a day off, followed by two days of brisk walking at the end of each week. Your walking time will increase each week so that by the end of the fourth week you will be walking aerobically for 45 minutes each time you walk.

To walk aerobically, you will need to calculate your target or training heart rate.

Your Target Heart Rate

Walking will improve your fitness even without checking your pulse. However, if you wish to have an aerobic workout and condition the heart, then you need to walk intensely enough to raise your heart-beat to between 60 per cent and 80 per cent of its maximum. (For the very unfit, 50–60 per cent is an adequate goal.)

This workout zone is known as the target, or training heart rate zone and experts believe that it is in this zone that substantial benefits are provided for cardiovascular and respiratory health. For most people, walking at a speed of 3.5–4 mph will be sufficient to achieve this. For some, however, a pace of 4.5 mph may be necessary to put them into their training zone.

There is an easy way to calculate your target heart rate zone. For example:

1. Subtract your age from 220. If you are 40 then that will be $220 - 40 = 180$. That's your maximum heart rate.
2. Now calculate 60 per cent and 80 per cent of your maximum heart rate: 180×60 per cent $= 108$ and 180×80 per cent $= 144$.

YOUR TARGET HEART RATE

AGE	MAXIMUM HEART RATE	60% LEVEL	80% LEVEL
20	200	120	160
25	195	117	156
30	190	114	152
35	185	111	148
40	180	108	144
45	175	105	140
50	170	102	136
55	165	99	132
60	160	96	128
65	155	93	124
70	150	90	120

TABLE 5

So, if you are 40 years old, your goal is to keep your pulse rate between 108 and 144 beats per minute when you are walking. Get into a good rhythm, say for five minutes or so, then check your pulse in the same way that you checked your resting pulse rate earlier. If you are below the lower end of your target range, then speed up a bit to bring yourself within it. If you are above the higher end of your target range, then slow down until you are back within your training zone again. Table 5 will help you see at a glance where your lower and upper personal target limits are without the need to calculate them yourself.

Knowing your pulse rate during exercise helps you stay in the 'target zone'. In this zone the heart and lungs must work hard to meet the body's increased demand for oxygen. If the exercise is performed for a minimum of 20 minutes, three or four times a week, then the exercise is sufficient to strengthen the heart muscle, increase the amount of blood in the body and improve your lung capacity. If you fail to reach the lower end of your 'target zone' for some reason, then you will still tone your muscles, burn away calories and improve your general health. But you will miss the real benefits that are available when you 'go aerobic'. Going aerobic is like changing gears in a car. The body suddenly begins to work more efficiently; it runs smoother, burns oxygen more efficiently, and you move into a new dimension.

As you measure your pulse rate over a period of weeks, you will have a good idea of the improvements you are making to your overall health and fitness. But don't let pulse taking make your workouts frustrating. Once you become experienced, you will be able to keep within your target zone simply by knowing how it feels. One way to do this – that is, to know how you 'perceive' it – is to use the following Rating of Perceived Exertion, or RPE, as recommended by Dr James Rippe, Director of the Exercise Physiology and Nutrition Laboratory at the University of Massachusetts Medical Center.

The RPE relies more on your feeling, or gut sense of how hard you are exercising, than on actually tracking your pulse rate. It works on the assumption that if you think you are getting a hard workout, then you probably are and your heart rate is likely to be in the aerobic target zone.

The RPE runs from 6 to 20. Each number represents a phase that describes your perception of how hard you are exercising. Six, for example, means 'no exertion'; 20 means 'maximum exertion'. By adding a zero to each number, you get a rough approximation of heart rate. For instance, an RPE of 12–13 represents a workout which is 'somewhat hard' in the target heart range of 120–130.

The RPE is a rough guide only and converting it to a heart rate is difficult for older people and for those out of condition. For older people, the maximum heart rate is much lower, and for those out of condition, even moderate exercise can set their heart-beats racing. But studies show that the RPE scale represents a close relationship between a person's perceived exertion during exercise and their actual heart rate.

RPE: Rating of Perceived Exertion	
Maximum exertion	20
Extremely Hard	19
	18
Very Hard	17
	16
Hard	15
	14
Somewhat Hard	13
	12
Light	11
	10
Very light	9
	8
Extremely Light	7
None	6

TABLE 6

WALKFIT – YOUR FOUR-WEEK FITNESS WALKING PROGRAMME

Days 1–7

The WALKFIT programme begins with Day 1. This can be any day of the week that you choose, but Monday is a good day to get started with something that is going to change the rest of your life. The plan is designed so that the final two days each week coincide with a weekend, when you are likely to have more time and energy to do fitness walking.

Begin with 20 minutes fitness walking. That means walking briskly around the route that you have measured out, and taking your pulse at regular intervals along the walk to make sure that you are within your target heart rate zone (your aerobic zone).

You will already have warmed up and stretched out, so you should now start gradually building your pace over four or five minutes, allowing your heart-beat to rise slowly into your target training zone. Walk with the longest stride that is comfortable. As your speed increases, your stride will lengthen and so will the distance that you cover. If you feel that you are straining, then reduce the pace until you feel comfortable again. It normally takes the first ten minutes of any walk to get into a good rhythm and get the circulation going, but once you get into your stride, you will find it easy to keep going.

The same rule for the WALKPLAN programme applies to the WALKFIT programme: if you can't hold a conversation while you walk, then you are going too fast.

Continue walking as per the WALKPLAN, filling the plan in each day to record your progress and keep you motivated.

WALKFIT

	Pace	Time Planned (Mins)	Time Walked (Mins)	Distance in Miles	Speed in m.p.h.	Comments
DAY 1	Brisk	20				
DAY 2	Moderate	20				
DAY 3	Brisk	20				
DAY 4	Moderate	20				
DAY 5	Rest day					
DAY 6	Brisk	20				
DAY 7	Brisk	20				
WEEKLY TOTALS						

TABLE 7

Days 8–14

This week you are gradually going to increase your time from 20 to 30 minutes each day. Make sure that you increase the time you walk before you increase your pace; get used to walking for longer before pushing yourself harder in your target heart rate zone.

As you walk each day, alternating moderate with brisk walking, gently stretch yourself to go a little further without tiring. At the end of the week you should be able to walk comfortably for 30 minutes at a brisk, aerobic level.

Days 15–21

You should now be beginning to feel the real benefits of fitness walking. Not only are your heart and lungs benefiting from your increased aerobic activity, but you are burning up calories while you walk. Walking a mile burns only about 10 to 20 per cent fewer calories than jogging a mile. For every mile you walk at 3.5 to 4 miles an hour, you are burning around 100 calories. You are becoming fitter and leaner.

This week you should gradually increase your walking time from 30 to 45 minutes. Again, make sure that you increase the time you walk *before* increasing your pace. This way you will find it easy to build on the previous day without overdoing it and getting injured in the process.

Days 22–28

Only seven more days and you will be a competent fitness walker. By the end of the third week you should have increased your walking time so that you are able to walk briskly for 45 minutes without tiring. Your fourth week

WALKFIT

	Pace	Time Planned (Mins)	Time Walked (Mins)	Distance in Miles	Speed in m.p.h.	Comments
DAY 8	Moderate	20–30				
DAY 9	Brisk	20–30				
DAY 10	Moderate	20–30				
DAY 11	Brisk	20–30				
DAY 12	Rest day					
DAY 13	Brisk	20–30				
DAY 14	Brisk	20–30				
WEEKLY TOTALS						

TABLE 8

WALKFIT

	Pace	Time Planned (Mins)	Time Walked (Mins)	Distance in Miles	Speed in m.p.h.	Comments
DAY 15	Moderate	30–45				
DAY 16	Brisk	30–45				
DAY 17	Moderate	30–45				
DAY 18	Brisk	30–45				
DAY 19	Rest day					
DAY 20	Brisk	30–45				
DAY 21	Brisk	30–45				
WEEKLY TOTALS						

TABLE 9

WALKFIT

	Pace	Time Planned (Mins)	Time Walked (Mins)	Distance in Miles	Speed in m.p.h.	Comments
DAY 22	Moderate	45				
DAY 23	Brisk	45				
DAY 24	Brisk	45				
DAY 25	Brisk	45				
DAY 26	Rest day					
DAY 27	Brisk	45				
DAY 28	Brisk	45				
WEEKLY TOTALS						

TABLE 10

begins with a moderate walk of 45 minutes, but after that it is fitness walking all the way to the end of your WALKFIT programme.

You should feel better, look better, and be motivated enough to carry on walking with the help of the WALKLIFE MAINTENANCE PROGRAMME. You will be burning around 300 calories each time you walk, and your increased metabolic rate will be helping to burn up another few hundred calories when you have finished walking.

HOW FAR, HOW FAST, HOW LONG?

As you will have already found, the easiest way to begin aerobic walking is to walk out of your own front door and do a circuit round the block and back – or around some other convenient route that is known to you. You will need to gauge the distances covered so the best way is to take a car ride around your proposed route and use the odometer to measure the distance between familiar landmarks.

As you build up your walking programme, you will need to increase the length of your circuit if you are going to cover sufficient miles. And you will need to measure it. Or you can simply cover as many circuits as you want around the same route in the way that athletes do circuit training on a track. And you will want to calculate your speed.

It is useful to remember the following formulae:

1. $\text{Distance} = \text{Speed} \times \text{Time}$
2. $\text{Speed} = \dfrac{\text{Distance}}{\text{Time}}$
3. $\text{Time} = \dfrac{\text{Distance}}{\text{Speed}}$

If you know any two of the variables above, it is easy to work out the third. Time is the easiest to measure; most people have a watch. So if you can measure the distance, it is then easy to calculate the speed.

Once you begin to stray from easily measured routes and landmarks, you will need to acquire a pedometer. A pedometer is a small gadget that clips on to your belt and which you adjust to the length of your own stride so that it measures the distance covered. With the help of your watch, it will also tell you the speed at which you are travelling. Pedometers can be purchased at most sports shops and large department stores.

There are two further methods of estimating the distance covered whilst walking.

Walking Speeds (mph)

Walk for one mile along the route you have previously measured with the car's odometer and time yourself. If it took you 15 minutes then you were walking at 4 mph.

$$\text{Speed} = \frac{\text{Distance}}{\text{Time}} = \frac{1 \text{ mile}}{0.25 \text{ hours}} = 4 \text{ mph}$$

As you vary your walking pace (increase your speed), then repeat the above method to calculate your new walking speed. You will soon get a feel for the speed you walk at and be able to judge different walking paces (2.5, 3.0, 3.5, 4.0 mph). If you can estimate your speed, and you know the time, then it is easy to work out the distance:

$$\text{Distance} = \text{Speed} \times \text{Time}$$

The Step Method

Count the number of steps that you take in one minute at your normal walking speed. Since the average stride is approximately two feet per step and there are 5,280 feet in one mile then it will take 2,640 steps to cover one mile. If your speed is 176 steps per minute then it will take 15 minutes to cover one mile:

$$\begin{aligned} \text{Distance} &= \text{Speed} \times \text{Time} \\ &= 176 \text{ steps/min} \times 15 \text{ mins} \\ &= 2{,}640 \text{ steps} \end{aligned}$$

You may want to measure your exact stride in the way that a pedometer does. To do this, measure the distance from toe to toe or heel to heel when you take a normal stride. The easiest way is to get someone to help you. Then calculate the distance walked in the same way as above.

Walking Speed Conversion Table

You can measure your speed with the help of a pedometer, or you can walk around a measured course. Another way is a variation of the step method above. To get a rough estimate of your speed, measure the length of your stride, then count how many steps you take per minute and compare the results with the following table:

Steps per minute			Minutes	Miles
2.0 ft/stride	2.5 ft/stride	3.0 ft/stride	per mile	per hour
90	70	60	30	2
110	90	75	24	2.5
130	105	90	20	3
155	120	105	17	3.5
175	140	120	15	4
200	160	135	13	4.5
220	175	145	12	5

TABLE 11

THE 15-MINUTE MILE

Once you have been using the WALKFIT programme for a while, striding out into your target heart rate zone, then try for the 15-minute mile. There is a sense of well-being that comes from achieving a goal, and when you can walk at 4 miles per hour for 15 minutes, you will feel that you have really achieved something.

Of course, some of you may easily be able to walk at this pace, but for many people, a speed of 3.5–4 miles per hour is sufficient to keep them within their aerobic heart range and to give them a vigorous workout. But only try for the 15-minute mile when you have gradually increased your pace from moderate to brisk and your body feels comfortable with the additional exertion.

As with all fitness walking, don't begin by walking too fast. Warm up first by increasing your pace gradually, then put your foot down. This will ensure that you accelerate safely without pushing your body into the injury zone.

Once you achieve the 15-minute mile, then try to walk two miles in 30 minutes, making sure that you gradually push yourself to achieve this. When you can comfortably do this, then your next goal is to walk three miles in 45 minutes.

The WALKFIT programme gradually increases your walking time from 20 to 45 minutes a day. It is important to increase the length of your workout before you increase the intensity so that you don't push too hard, too soon. So please don't try and increase your speed until you feel ready for it.

GETTING INTO THE SWING OF IT

* *Your walking centre* – If you imagine a straight line going down the road between the centre of your feet and stretching ahead of you, then this represents your walking centre. Keeping your legs parallel to this line and your toes pointing directly ahead, walk with your normal stride.

* *Finding your stride* – Pace is the key to finding your stride and reaching a good rhythm in your walking. Set off at a good pace with the longest stride that is comfortable, letting your arms swing naturally in opposition to your feet.

The arms should move at the same speed as the legs. If you relax your shoulders, then as you walk the arms will swing by themselves, finding their own natural rhythm. As your right foot swings forwards, your left arm will swing with it; when your left foot swings forwards, your right arm will swing in opposition to it. The arms and shoulders move and swing in a pendulum-like motion in counterbalance to the legs and hips.

As you walk faster, you will find that your arms bend naturally and quicken up to keep pace with your legs. There is no need to pump the arms aggressively backwards and forwards, bent at a 90-degree angle. This technique has more to do with race walking and power walking than it does with genuine fitness walking. Fitness walking is a moderate activity which anyone can enjoy – not just athletes and those who follow the 'no pain, no gain' way.

* *Heel to toe* – You will want to make sure that your feet are landing in the right place, and the way to do this is to use the heel-toe method. As you step from one foot to the other, the heel of your leading foot should touch the ground just before the ball of the foot and toes. Then as the heel touches the ground, lock your ankle and shift your weight forwards with the knee bent, rocking on to the toes and using them to push you off to the next step.

* *Breathe naturally* – As you build up to a steady pace, your breathing should deepen naturally and you should inhale and exhale rhythmically through the nose. If you normally breathe from the chest area rather than the abdomen, try breathing deeply from the abdomen. Efficient breathing through the nostrils pulls the air down deep into the lungs, expanding the lungs downwards and the lungs and chest forwards. To breathe deeply, inhale by first moving your abdomen outwards. You will feel your stomach rise, then your upper abdomen, and finally your chest. Then breathe out by letting your stomach relax.

Deep rhythmic breathing will revitalise you. Your muscles will relax and your mind will clear, as tension and stress are drained away and you let go totally.

YOUR WALKFIT COOL-DOWN

It is as important to cool down after fitness walking as it is to warm up for it beforehand. Don't just stop walking; gently reduce your pace over four or five minutes as you come to the end of your walk. This will help you to avoid post-exercise stiffness and sore muscles, and help return your heart and blood pressure back to a normal level. It will also help prevent potential pooling of blood in the legs, which can reduce blood flow to the head, causing slight dizziness.

As soon as your walk is over, you should follow through with a few cooling-down exercises. Time spent gently stretching is actually more effective at the end of your workout, since your muscles and tendons are already warm and loose and can be stretched further.

Repeat the side and shoulder stretches and the 'reach for the sky' stretch from your warm-up routine and if you have time, finish with the 'total relaxation' pose as shown in Chapter 5.

Apart from the time spent fitness walking, you may find that one of the most pleasurable times of the day is after you have finished walking, done your stretching exercises, and you can just lie back and relax in the 'total relaxation' pose.

YOUR WALKLIFE MAINTENANCE PROGRAMME

If one just keeps on walking everything will be all right.

SOREN KIERKEGAARD

When you have finished the WALKFIT programme, give yourself a pat on the back. You deserve it. You've learnt a new skill. You will have lost weight, be more supple and have more stamina to help you through the day. And you will be well on the way to developing cardiovascular fitness and long-term health. Exercise is for life, and we hope that we have now proved to you that it can be easy and it can be fun.

All you have to do now is to keep it up – keep up the motivation and keep walking regularly. Although you've done the hardest part – working through the previous programmes and getting into shape – none of the walking will have done you any real good if you don't continue with it. And that's where the WALKLIFE MAINTENANCE PROGRAMME can help. From now on, the goals are going to be set by you.

The WALKLIFE programme now builds on what you've already accomplished. Your success will depend on keeping up the frequency and intensity of your walks each week. To maintain and continue cardiovascular and respiratory fitness your minimum programme is to walk for 30 minutes four times a week in your target training zone. This is the amount of time that most regular runners put in each week and is more than the minimum recommended time suggested by the British Heart Foundation and the Aerobics Institute in the USA.

You can achieve a lot in 30 minutes. It's enough to give you a vigorous workout, leaving time for warming up and cooling down, and it will allow you to get into your stride and set a good rhythm for your walk. Once you have built up a rhythm, you will find it easier to walk for the last ten minutes than you will for the first ten. And if you feel like going on further, then do so. Your body is the best judge. No one knows it like you do. Listen to it; it is always right.

Do your fitness walking on alternate days. Muscles that are being worked hard usually take 48 hours to recover; but there is no reason why you can't walk moderately on the days between fitness workouts. As long as you are achieving a minimum of 30 minutes fitness walking four times a week, then you can walk at other times for different reasons – for slimness, for relaxation, to de-stress, or simply for the fun of it.

Filling in the WALKLIFE programme will continue to keep you motivated, and along with your walking diary it will provide you with essential information about your achievements. The programme has been left blank so that it can be photocopied and used again. Fill in the days to suit, and keep a record of your time planned, time walked, distance, speed, weekly totals and comments about your walks.

Keep walking.

WALKFIT

Date	Time Planned (Mins)	Time Walked (Mins)	Distance in Miles	Speed in m.p.h.	Comments
WEEKLY TOTALS					

TABLE 12

CHAPTER FIVE

WALKING
And Total Fitness

That which is used develops. That which is not used wastes away.

HIPPOCRATES

Many people starting out with a fitness programme are looking for the one activity that will solve all their problems – develop stamina, suppleness and strength, help with weight control, and develop cardiovascular fitness. Sadly, no one exercise can do all of this for them – not even fitness walking.

Although fitness walking exercises the main muscle mass of the body, gives you a good cardiovascular work-out and develops respiratory efficiency, it cannot give you all the exercise required for total body fitness, and it's a total fitness approach that you need if you are going to develop a fit, healthy body.

A total fitness approach provides you with the three basics of fitness – stretching, strength training and aerobic conditioning. But the benefits do not end with physical fitness. Total fitness stretches you physically, emotionally and psychologically; it helps you to explore your body and get the most out of it; it helps you to get to know yourself better.

We are not asking you to carry weights when you walk, pump weights or spend hours every week in the gym. All you need to do is follow this simple work-out routine three or four times a week to develop the long-term fitness benefits that will supplement your walking routine.

Using the following simple exercises will help you to loosen up the body and stretch it. Stretching improves circulation, improves the mobility of joints, assists in developing correct posture and prevents problems such as lower back pain.

Begin your work-out by warming up. You will remember from the last chapter just how important warming up is. And this applies as much to the following exercises as it does to fitness walking. It's estimated that 80 per cent of injuries could be avoided with proper preparation. Warm-ups pump blood into the muscles and help with the lubrication of joints.

Unless you are following through with these exercises after fitness walking, in which case you will have already done warm-up and cool-down exercises, you should begin with brisk walking on the spot. Follow the warm-up routine in Chapter 4, omitting the exercises that specifically assist walking – the ankle, hamstring, Achilles and quadriceps stretches. You will be doing enough of these in your pre-walk warm-ups. Then continue with the total fitness exercises, always ending with the total relaxation pose which will help you to quietly collect your thoughts.

READ THE FOLLOWING CAREFULLY

If you have been sedentary for some time, you are likely to be stiff and out of condition, so you should approach the exercises with caution. And if you have a specific back, neck or other problem that may prevent you from performing any of the movements, then you should consult your family doctor before trying them – show him the exercises and ask his advice. This applies if you are pregnant as well – consult your doctor first.

As you perform the exercises, your movements should flow naturally. Don't overstretch; don't force yourself. Keep within your ability and always listen to your own body – it is always right. As you perform each exercise, slowly stretch into the position, going only as far as is comfortable. If it begins to hurt then ease back or stop. When you have completed the exercise, come out of it slowly.

The key is to progress gradually so that your flexibility and strength improve without straining yourself. Fitness walking is a moderate, low-stress exercise which allows you to build up an aerobic routine without straining yourself. The total fitness exercises are also designed as a moderate, low-stress routine which gradually allows you to increase the time that you hold a pose, or the number of repetitions that you make.

All the exercises are shown at full extension, so if you are unfit you should take particular care to build gradually towards the full exercise. The number of repetitions for each exercise and the length of time that poses are held are meant only as a guide – if necessary, reduce them to what you find comfortable. Similarly, as you progress week by week, you may wish to increase the intensity of the exercises to suit yourself. If you find any exercise too difficult to begin with, then leave it out until you gain the necessary strength and suppleness to approach it again. Take particular care with the strengthening exercises – push-ups, triceps and pectorals stretches. It is easy to overdo them. If necessary, begin with wall push-ups, graduating later to floor push-ups. If you listen to your body, you will not go far wrong.

As you exercise, try to be aware of the movements that you are making. Concentrate on each movement and the effect that the exercise is having on a particular muscle group. Visualise the beneficial effects – see the muscles loosening, stretching and strengthening. To breathe correctly, exhale through the mouth on the effort then inhale through the nose and mouth as muscles are released.

When should you do the exercises? Do them after fitness walking; do them before eating; never do them until at least 90 minutes after a meal. Do them on a morning; do them on an evening. Vary the times so that you do not become bored. Do some of them at work when you feel stiff, tired and tense.

Total fitness is a defence against fatigue, depression and stress. It helps strengthen and tone your entire body, restoring balance, poise and self-confidence. It leaves you feeling refreshed and revitalised, ready to cope with anything that life offers.

1. CHEST AND BUST FIRMER
To strengthen arms, shoulders, back and chest

Hold your wrists at shoulder-height in front of you. Grip as if pushing
each hand towards the opposite elbow. Hold for 10 seconds then release.
Repeat 3 times.

2. TRICEP STRETCH
To stretch and tone the triceps and upper back

Raise arms and bend right elbow so that the right hand rests on the upper
back. Hold right elbow with left hand and gently pull the right elbow in
towards your head until you feel a slight stretching sensation in the back
of your arm and across the upper back and shoulders. Hold for 10 seconds.
Repeat 3 times and change arms.

3. CHEST STRETCH
To stretch out the pectorals and upper arms

Stand with your feet apart. Clasp hands behind back then gently raise
them, keeping your elbows slightly bent the whole time. Hold for 8
seconds. Relax and repeat.

4. WALL PUSH-UPS
To strengthen and develop the arm, shoulder and chest muscles

Stand about 3 feet from a wall. Raise arms to shoulder-height and place
on wall. Slowly bend arms as much as you can to the count of 3. Then
return to starting position to the count of 3 and repeat 10 times.

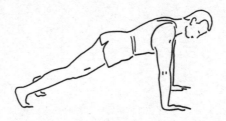

5. PUSH-UPS
To strengthen arms, shoulders, back and chest

Lie face down, palms flat beside shoulders and toes tucked under. Breathe
in, then, breathing out, push up as far as possible. Breathe in and lower
to a couple of inches above the floor. Repeat 5–10 times.

6. LOWER BACK STRETCH
To stretch out the hamstrings, inner thighs and back

Lie flat on back, knees bent, feet flat. Pull one knee towards you gently
until you feel a slight stretch in the back of the thigh. Hold for 15–20
seconds. Repeat with other leg.

a.

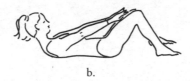

b.

7. CURL-UPS
To strengthen stomach and back

a. Lie on back, knees bent with feet and knees hip-width apart. Place
hands lightly on stomach. Press your back to the floor.

b. Slowly curl up from the stomach and raise shoulders and head a couple
of inches, reaching with both hands towards knees. Gently lower. Breathe
out going up, and in going down. Repeat 5 times, pause, then repeat 5
times.

8. ELEVATED SIT-UPS
To strengthen abdomen, back and neck

Lie on your back, feet pointing to ceiling, knees slightly bent, arms by your sides. Using abdominal muscles, raise head and upper torso, exhaling as you reach forward with hands past your thighs. Inhale and relax back without letting head touch floor. Repeat 5 times.

9. SCISSORS
To firm up stomach and thighs

Lie on back with knees bent, feet flat on floor. Raise one leg at a time, keeping small of back pressed flat on to floor. Then make scissor movement in air 5 times. Lower legs one at a time again and repeat from start 5 times. Don't arch your back, and keep neck and spine in line.

10. LEG LIFTS

To strengthen abdomen, thighs and lower back

Lie on your back, arms outstretched. Slowly raise then lower each leg alternately, counting 5 to raise, 5 to hold and 5 to lower. Don't arch your back. Repeat 5 times, relaxing between.

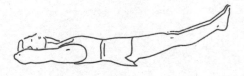

11. LEG RAISES

To strengthen abdomen, thighs and lower back

Lie on your back, legs together, arms behind your head. Keeping legs straight, raise feet gently from floor a few inches, keeping small of back pressed down on floor. Hold for 5–10 seconds. Repeat 5 times.

a.

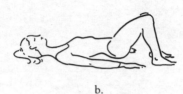

b.

12. BACK PUSH-UP
To strengthen middle of back and shoulders and firm up thighs and buttocks

a.   Lie flat on floor, knees bent, arms by your side. Pull your stomach in and breathe deeply from abdomen for 10 seconds, keeping lower back pressed flat.

b.   Then lift buttocks off floor by contracting them and using your stomach muscles. Hold for 5 seconds. Repeat 5 times.

13. SITTING TOE TOUCHES
To stretch the inner thighs, spine, hamstrings, shoulders and back

Sit on floor, legs straight out in front, feet together, backs of knees touching the floor. Very slowly reach forward from the waist as far as is comfortable, clasping the calves, and keeping the spine and neck long. Hold for 10 seconds. Repeat 3 times.

14. WAISTLINE FIRMER

To tone and strengthen inside and outside thighs, back and abdomen

a.   From legs together position, slowly raise top leg as far as you can. Hold for count of 5, then slowly lower. Repeat 5 times.

a.

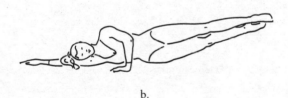

b.

b.   Keeping legs together, slowly raise them. Hold for count of 5 then slowly lower. Repeat 5 times. Turn over and repeat both movements, 5 times each.

15. INNER THIGH STRETCH
To stretch out the groin area

Sit with the soles of your feet together and as close to you as is comfortable.
Keep your back straight. Hold your ankles and press your knees downwards.
Hold for 10 seconds then release. Repeat 3 times.

16. LOWER BACK STRETCH
To stretch out the lower back, and inside and back of thighs

Sit up with left leg straight and right leg bent. Gently lean over the left leg
from the hips until you feel a slight stretching sensation down the back
of the outstretched leg. Hold for 10 seconds. Repeat 3 times, alternating
legs.

17. SPINAL STRETCH
To stretch out lower back and side of hip

Sit, legs outstretched. Place right foot over left leg, then place right hand behind you and left hand across your body for support. Slowly twist to right. Stretch body and turn head gently to side. Do 3 twists then change over legs; left foot over right leg and repeat exercise.

18. BACK STRENGTHENER
To strengthen the lower back

Lie face down on floor with hands under thighs. Gently lift head a couple of inches, hold and relax. Don't arch your back. Repeat 5 times.

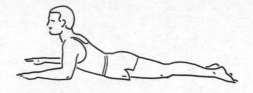

19. THE COBRA
To mobilise the spine and strengthen the back

Lie face down, palms flat on the floor at shoulder-height with elbows
tucked into sides. Gently push up until you are resting on your elbows.
Keep your spine and neck in line, still watching the floor so that you don't
twist neck. Hold for 10 seconds then relax. Repeat 5 times.

20. BACK STRETCH
To stretch out the centre of the back, and tone and strengthen
the thighs, buttocks, shoulders, arms and abdomen

Lie on back with knees bent and feet flat. Raise arms out to shoulder-
height and bend at elbows so that the backs of the hands are flat on the
floor. Don't arch your back. Bring your right leg over the left, lowering
the knee towards the floor. Hold for 10 seconds. Repeat on other side.

21. TOTAL RELAXATION

Lie flat on back, knees bent, arms at sides and support the back of head
with books piled to a height of about 4 inches. Breathe deeply from
abdomen and concentrate on relaxing every part of the body. Start with
the toes and say to yourself 'my toes are completely and totally relaxing'.
Work up through the rest of the body: the legs, stomach, chest, back,
shoulders, to the head, using the same relaxing words, but using your
own version. A total relaxation session can last from 5 to 15 minutes or
longer.

CHAPTER SIX

THE FITNESS WALKER'S DIET
The Shape of Things to Come

Tell me what you eat and I will tell you what you are.

BRILLAT-SAVARIN

THE FATS OF LIFE

You are what you eat.

Leading health experts and nutritionists all agree that sensible eating habits and nutritious foods are the way to looking good and feeling great – the way to health, energy and vitality. Paying attention to your diet isn't about forbidden foods, calorie-counting and self-denial. It's more a question of self-knowledge: giving thought to the food you eat, and giving a higher profile to some foods rather than others.

Studies show that 60 per cent of all deaths are from conditions related to the food we eat. And, according to recent research, 35 per cent of all cancer deaths and 80 per cent of cardiovascular disease in the United Kingdom may be related to diet. Similarly, in the USA, the National Cancer Institute and the American Heart Association advise that dietary changes must be made to reduce the risk of chronic disease. Here, too, they estimate that 40 per cent of cancer incidence in men and almost 60 per cent in women is diet-related. And diet is implicated in two major factors leading to heart disease – high blood pressure and high blood cholesterol levels.

The relationship between diet and disease is now widely accepted and there is a consensus among experts as to which dietary elements play a role in the development of disease. One of the main ones is fat – and of all the changes you can make in your diet, cutting down on fat, particularly saturated fat, will have the greatest effect on reducing your risk of disease.

Fat has been quoted in the USA Surgeon General's 'Nutrition and Health' report as Western society's greatest nutritional hazard. Each gram contains nine calories whereas a protein or carbohydrate gram contains only four. At more than twice the calories, gram for gram, an excessive intake of fat can lead to obesity and an increased risk of certain forms of cancer.

But cutting back on fat is only one change you can make in your diet. Another major change is to cut back on salt and sugar.

THE FAT CATS WHO SUGAR YOUR DIET

* In Britain we eat £2.4 billion worth of chocolate a year
* We spend £1.2 billion a year on snacks, and the market is growing by 20 per cent a year
* We spend £1 billion a year on scones, teacakes, cream cakes, eclairs, chocolate cakes and Swiss rolls

None of these items plays any part in a balanced, nutritious diet, and if you eliminated them all, it is likely that you would live a longer, healthier life, and one free from disease. But if you want to give them up, or even cut down on them, you will have an uphill battle, because the purveyors of these items spend £200 million a year persuading us to buy their products. In comparison, the Health Education Authority spends £4 million a year on nutritional messages. With such fat profits to be made, is it any wonder that the junk food industry continues to sugar its messages to the public?

But surely there is some nutritional value in chocolate, cakes and snacks? Well ... some! But compare for yourself the nutritional value of the following:

a small 2 oz chocolate bar contains:
25 g of fat (mainly saturated)
17 g of refined sugar
0.1 g of dietary fibre
300 calories

a medium size pear contains:
0.7 g of fat
4.5 g of dietary fibre
80 calories (the sugar it contains is fructose – fruit sugar)

You shouldn't expect too much from the purveyors of snacks, chocolates, cakes and the like. After all, their prime interest is not in the nutritional value of their foods; it is in the 'added value' of their foods. Added value, or value added, is the new economic buzz phrase for profit. To the social engineers and the marketing men who manipulate your taste buds through advertising, the idea of profit may offend, but 'value added' conjures up a sense of a caring, desirable product.

The truth is that there's not much profit to be made out of an apple or a pear; but there is a lot of money to be made out of fatty, sugary, salty products gift wrapped and marketed to a gullible public. Their 'value added' products are in reality 'fat added', 'sugar added' and 'salt added'. And fat, sugar and salt are the deadly trio that attack our bodies. We have already seen that fat is the single greatest dietary health hazard. But sugar has been called 'pure, white and deadly', and salt has been identified by the *British Medical Journal* as causing up to 75,000 deaths a year.

To inflame matters further, the Western nations are eating more processed foods than ever before – in Britain alone, 20 million fast foods are eaten every week. And fast food usually means fat food, sugared food, salty, high-cholesterol, high-calorie food. A hamburger can contain up to 15 teaspoonfuls of fat, 1 g of salt and 1,000 calories. And a large chocolate milk-shake can contain up to 30 teaspoonfuls of sugar and 1,000 calories. Is it surprising then that almost six million people in Britain are obese – about 20 per cent or more over their ideal body weight – and more than 100,000 people suffer from extreme obesity, at which point it is thought medically essential to lose weight? You might think that no one was interested in trying to lose weight – but the facts speak for themselves.

THE DIET REVOLUTION

Dieting has never been more popular. At any one time in the UK, one in four people is on a diet, 40 per cent of British men and 32 per cent of British women are overweight (almost 21 million people in total), and the slimming industry is

A HEALTHY BALANCE

Increase your intake of:

OILY FISH

kippers	mackerel
herrings	pilchards
sardines	anchovies
tuna	salmon

WHITE FISH

haddock	cod
plaice	sole
hake	monkfish

VEGETABLES

peas	spinach	cabbage	sprouts
cauliflower	carrots	beetroot	potatoes
broccoli	leeks	celery	celeriac
French beans	runner beans	broad beans	parsnips
mushrooms	sweetcorn	turnips	swede
watercress	peppers	lettuce	cucumber

FRUIT

apples	pears	bananas	grapes
grapefruit	oranges	lemons	limes
pineapple	lychees	mango	guava
passion fruit	pomegranates	figs	dates
apricots	peaches	nectarines	melon
raspberries	strawberries	blackberries	tomatoes

STAPLE FOODS

wholemeal bread	wholegrain rice	wholemeal pasta	cereals
seeds	nuts	lentils	beans

WATER

Drink plenty of water – mineral water is readily available for those who prefer it. Water regulates body temperature and assists in all bodily functions.

TABLE 14A

Decrease your intake of:

SATURATED FATS

red meat	bacon	sausages	burgers
liver sausage	salami	luncheon meat	liver
butter	cheese	full-fat milk	cream

OILS AND FATS

coconut oil	palm oil	dripping	lard

REFINED CARBOHYDRATES

sugar	biscuits	cakes	pies
sweets	chocolate	puddings	pastries
desserts	white bread	gateaux	croissants

SNACKS

cheesy biscuits	crisps	peanuts	samosas
pastries	sausage rolls	ice-ream	pizzas

SALT

ALCOHOL

maximum: 3 units per day for men
2 units per day for women
1 unit = 1 glass of wine
half-pint beer
small measure spirits

Drink more low-alcohol or soft drinks – cut out alcohol altogether if so desired

COFFEE

Drink fewer cups of coffee or weaker blends

TEA

Drink less tea – try herb tea or fruit teas

TABLE 14B

THE DIET PYRAMID

SUGAR
(REFINED)

DAIRY
PRODUCTS AND OILS

EGGS AND
LEAN RED MEAT

FISH, SEAFOOD AND
WHITE MEAT

BREAD, POTATOES
PASTA AND CEREALS

VEGETABLES, SALADS AND FRUIT

TABLE 13

currently worth about £1 billion annually. In the USA, 100 million people spend $33 billion annually on diets and diet-related products. Yet generally, only 5 per cent of the people keep up with a diet and are successful. Clearly, the traditional method of dieting is not the way to reduce weight and build long-term health. So what is the way?

Making permanent changes in your eating habits rather than 'going on a diet' is the key to it. The traditional diet is a short-term crash-course, while healthy eating based on sound nutrition is a long-term strategy designed to make permanent changes in your lifestyle.

Crash diets fool your body into thinking that it is being starved. The body's metabolic rate is then slowed down, as it would be in time of real famine, and it actually conserves fat. And although you may have an initial weight-loss, as soon as you increase your intake of calories, your weight will also increase. It is so easy with this form of dieting to become obsessed with food, making it an even greater priority than it was before.

Counting calories places too great an emphasis on food – as well as being extremely boring! The important thing is to be aware of the nutritional content of what you eat, and particularly the fat content, as it's the fat you eat that makes you fat.

HOW TO DO THE FITNESS WALKER'S DIET

At the beginning of this chapter, we suggested that the best way to control what you eat is to give a higher profile to some foods rather than others. The balanced diet pyramid in

Table 13 does just this. Nothing has to be forbidden. Don't think in terms of foods being good or bad; simply as foods to increase and decrease (see Tables 14a and 14b – A Healthy Balance).

The pyramid shows the key action areas for a balanced diet. You can eat as much as you like from foods at the base of the pyramid – vegetables, salads and fruit – but you should aim for at least 400 g each day. You can then add foods to that foundation from further up the pyramid – bread, potatoes, pasta and cereals. The foods on these first two levels of the pyramid should form the cornerstone of your FITNESS WALKER'S DIET.

As you work your way up the pyramid, you can add protein in the form of fish and seafood, which is a good low-fat source of vitamins and minerals. And you can add moderate amounts of white meat – chicken and turkey – since it is lower in fat than red meat.

As you get towards the top of the pyramid, you should be trying to reduce or substitute these foods, as they should only play a small role in a balanced, nutritious diet. Red meat is higher in fat than white meat, and dairy products are all high in fat so should be used sparingly. Refined sugar, at the top of the pyramid, should be reduced to the bare minimum, and you should watch out for hidden sugar in the form of confectionery: buns, cakes, eclairs etc.

Meat and fish are often the main part of a meal in the Western diet with vegetables or pasta as merely a garnish. It should be the reverse of this – try cooking meals in which the meat or fish is more of an accompaniment, with the main emphasis on vegetables or salad, rice or pasta.

To help you work out where you should make changes in your diet, and to maintain your new healthy way of eating, it is a good idea to keep a food diary. Like the walking

FOOD DIARY

Week beginning:	BREAKFAST	LIGHT MEAL	MAIN MEAL	EXTRAS
Monday				
Tuesday				
Wednesday				
Thursday				
Friday				
Saturday				
Sunday				

TABLE 15

diary which you will have started in your WALKPLAN programme, it will give you the information that you need in a concise form, and it will help to keep you motivated. Table 15 is a good example. For the first week write down everything that you have eaten. Compare this with the balanced diet pyramid and then, with help from the rest of this chapter, work out where and how you should make your changes.

Try to balance your diet over a week. And always have plenty of variety in your meals – never before have the shops had such a wealth of foods to choose from (see Table 16).

FIVE GOLDEN RULES FOR HEALTHY EATING

* Eat fresh foods – keep away from processed foods

* Increase your intake of fibre – eat lots of fresh fruit and vegetables, cereals, pulses and grains

* Cut right down on fats – particularly saturated fats

* Decrease your intake of sugar and salt – try other flavourings

* Add variety to your diet – make use of the many different vegetables, fruit and fish now available

---

TABLE 16

A balanced diet should maintain health, provide energy, promote growth and give protection against disease. Our total energy consumption should come from the following food sources (report by the UK National Advisory Committee on Nutritional Education):

Carbohydrate	55 per cent
Fat	30 per cent
Protein	11 per cent
Alcohol	4 per cent

Carbohydrate

The function of carbohydrates – compounds of carbon, hydrogen and oxygen – is to provide energy. There are two types of carbohydrate – simple and complex. Simple carbohydrates are very quickly digested whereas complex ones are digested slowly, providing more energy and stamina. Of our daily energy intake, 55 per cent should come from carbohydrates, particularly complex, unrefined ones such as wholegrains, potatoes and other vegetables.

Sugar, a simple, refined carbohydrate, provides energy but hardly any nutrients. Our intake of sugar does not consist solely of what we put in tea or coffee – many people have now given up having sugar in this way – and much is hidden in processed foods such as cakes, soft drinks and chocolate. Eating these provides calories without much added nutritional value.

On the other hand, calories in foods high in complex carbohydrates usually contain a lot of nutritional extras. For example, two slices of wholewheat bread contain about 130 calories, the calorie-count for a soft drink. However, the bread also contains protein, fibre and a small amount of calcium and iron. None of these are to be found in a soft drink.

WHERE THE FIBRE IS

	VEGETABLES	FRUIT	OTHER
VERY HIGH	peas red kidney beans	dried apricots dried figs dried prunes passion fruit	wheatbran cornflakes yeast almonds
HIGH	baked beans spinach	blackberries blackcurrants redcurrants raspberries dried dates dried raisins dried sultanas	wholemeal flour/bread oatmeal brazil nuts chestnuts peanuts
MEDIUM	beans – French broad butter runner cabbage cerliac leeks mushrooms jacket potatoes	apples bananas cranberries pears damsons	white flour/bread pitta bread wholemeal spaghetti walnuts

VERY HIGH over 10g per 100g

carrots
beetroot
lentils
broccoli
sprouts
parsnips
sweetcorn
watercress

MEDIUM over 2g per 100g

LOW

asparagus
celery
aubergine
cauliflower
cucumber
lettuce
onions
courgettes
peppers

HIGH over 6g per 100g

gooseberries
nectarines
plums
rhubarb
strawberries

LOW under 2g per 100g

cherries
grapes
mango
lychees
grapefruit
pineapple
tangerines
peaches
oranges
melon

TABLE 17

Fibre

Fibre is unrefined carbohydrate and can be found in such things as bread, potatoes, fruit, vegetables, nuts and pulses. Foods differ in the amount and type of fibre they contain, but all forms are resistant to human digestive enzymes, passing through the digestive tract without being completely broken down – nearly all other basic foods are digested. Fibre does not provide the body with any nutrients, but it does perform other valuable functions and there are two types of it – soluble and insoluble.

Soluble fibre is to be found in fruit, vegetables, seeds and oats, and helps reduce blood cholesterol levels and may decrease the likelihood of cardiovascular disease. It may also slow down the entry of glucose into the bloodstream which is particularly valuable for diabetics.

Insoluble fibre can be found in whole grains and on the outside of fruit and seeds. The outer part is often the chewiest and is invariably removed in the processing of foods, but this part should be eaten as it promotes the more efficient elimination of waste from the body and may help in some digestive disorders.

Because of the general preference for high-protein and sugary foods rather than fruit, vegetables and whole grains, the intake of fibre in the average Western diet has decreased at the same time that many Western diseases and physical problems have increased – constipation, intestinal disorders, cancer, heart disease, gallstones, diabetes and obesity. In contrast, research among rural Africans has shown that there is a low incidence of all of these, which may be helped or prevented by their high fibre intake.

You should eat at least 30 g of fibre daily. If you wish to increase your fibre intake, it is best to do so gradually so that your system can adjust to the addition of fibre-rich foods. Eat less processed food and eat more fruit and vegetables, leaving the skin on whenever possible. Not only are fruit and vegetables low-calorie sources of fibre but they are also rich in vitamins and minerals. Drink plenty of liquid (see Table 14a) and eat foods high in fibre at every meal (see Table 17 – Where the Fibre Is).

Fat

Generally the amount of fat we eat should be reduced. No more than 30 per cent of our daily calories should come from it. And it is not only a matter of cutting the fat from meat, but also being aware of the hidden fats in food – in cakes, chocolate and sauces, for example.

Saturated fat in particular should be reduced. It should make up less than 10 per cent of your daily calorie intake because it can cause high blood cholesterol levels which clog the arteries and may lead to a heart attack or stroke. Saturated fat is found in animal products – red meat, cheese, milk, cream and butter. Try using the widely available alternatives: skimmed or semi-skimmed milk, low-fat yogurt and margarine low in saturated fats. And eat more white meat and fish (see Table 18 – Substitutes).

Fish is an excellent source of Omega-3 fatty acids which can help prevent clogging of the arteries and heart disease. These fish oils are found in mackerel, herrings, pilchards, sardines, tuna, trout and salmon. There is a very low record of heart disease among Greenland Eskimos because of the amount of fish they eat. The best advice now available is to increase our intake of Omega-3 fish oils and reduce our intake of Omega-6 fats found in animal products (see Table 19 – Where the Fat Is).

SUBSTITUTES

Instead of:	use:
full-fat milk	skimmed or semi-skimmed milk
butter	margarine high in poly-unsaturates
cream	natural yogurt or reduced fat cream
cream- or cheese-based sauces	yogurt- or tomato-based sauces
salad dressing or mayonnaise	lemon juice, lime juice or reduced calorie mayonnaise
red meat	white meat or fish
fried foods	grilled, steamed or poached foods
high-protein and high-fat meals	high-fibre meals
starters	crudités
puddings	low-fat yogurt or fresh fruit
salt	fresh herbs as flavouring
snacks such as crisps, biscuits and cakes	fresh fruit or crudités
alcoholic drinks	low-alcohol drinks or mineral water
fizzy drinks	low-calorie drinks
tea and coffee	fresh fruit or vegetable juices

TABLE 18

WHERE THE FAT IS

VERY HIGH liver sausage, salami, sausage rolls, whitebait – fried, chocolate, crisps, biscuits, cakes, pastry, cheesecake, butter, cream, cheese, cream cheese, lard, vegetable oils, French dressing, mayonnaise, almonds, brazil nuts, pistachio nuts, peanuts, marzipan

HIGH bacon, roast duck, roast goose, sausages – grilled, anchovies, tuna – canned in oil, scampi – fried, avocado pear, croissants, pasty, chips, doughnuts, éclairs, pancakes, toffees, fried eggs, cheese sauce

MEDIUM roast beef, roast lamb, roast pork, roast chicken (with skin), roast turkey (with skin), pheasant, venison, corned beef, fried haddock, fried cod in batter, herring, kipper, salmon, Greek yogurt, eggs

LOW chicken cooked without fat, turkey cooked without fat, grouse, cod – steamed, haddock – steamed, tuna – fresh, tuna – canned in brine, trout, prawns, bread – wholemeal or white, spaghetti, crème caramel, semi-skimmed milk, cottage cheese, low-fat yogurt, chestnuts

VERY HIGH	over 25g per 100g	**HIGH**	over 15g per 100g
MEDIUM	over 6g per 100g	**LOW**	under 6g per 100g

TABLE 19

Protein

Protein is the body's cell-builder and is found in fish, meat, pulses and beans. Although it is recommended that 11 per cent of our diet should be protein, we generally eat twice as much as we need – and excess protein is stored as fat. Again we should cut down on red meat and eat more white meat and fish. As vegetable protein (with the exception of that found in soya beans) lacks some of the eight essential amino acids which are found in animal proteins and are needed for good health, eggs should be included in our diet. Eggs contain all of the essential amino acids and are also an extremely versatile food.

Vitamins and Minerals

Vitamins and minerals, vital for growth and health, are natural substances that cannot be manufactured by our body; so we need to ensure that we follow a balanced diet which provides us with enough of them.

Vitamins are either water- or fat-soluble. Water-soluble vitamins are the B group (B_1, B_2, B_3, B_5, B_6 and B_{12}) and vitamin C. The fat-soluble ones are vitamins A, D, E and K. The B vitamins, or 'stress vitamins' as they are sometimes known, are found in staple foods – such as wholemeal bread, brown rice, pulses, nuts and grains – and in meat, fish, eggs, milk, poultry, green vegetables, bananas and cheese. They give protection against infection, aid in energy production, promote growth and are essential for a healthy nervous system.

Vitamin C is found in green, leafy vegetables, potatoes, tomatoes, fruits and berries. It is important for the growth and repair of cells, gums, blood vessels, bones and teeth and helps in healing disease – and is very important for smokers and those under stress. As the B and C vitamins are water-soluble, they cannot be stored in the body and must be replaced daily.

The fat-soluble vitamins, however, can be stored. They are to be found in root and green vegetables, cheese, milk, eggs, fish, fish oils, dairy foods, nuts and cereals. They promote growth, give protection against infection and are essential for other body functions.

The important minerals are calcium, zinc, iron, potassium, magnesium, phosphorous and iodine, whilst others required by the body are selenium, manganese, sodium and other trace elements. They can be found in milk, cheese, soya beans, seafood, poultry, green vegetables, meat, eggs, nuts, seeds, beans, oat bran, citrus fruits, apples, bananas and potatoes.

You can see how important it is to follow a balanced diet for a healthy life (use the Shopping List in Table 20 as a guide). Remember – you are what you eat!

Herbs and Spices – for Added Variety

There are many herbs and spices you can use to enhance the flavour of your food – and using them is a good way of reducing your intake of salt. The food should not be over-powered by the herbs or spices; rather, their addition should give subtle flavouring to your recipes. Try to use different herbs and spices in addition to those you already know. Nowadays there is so much variety available in local supermarkets and delicatessens.

SHOPPING LISTS

The following lists are a guide to what you should be buying for a balanced, healthy diet as suggested in THE FITNESS WALKER'S DIET:

FISH

kippers, herrings, mackerel, cod, haddock, salmon, tuna, hake, plaice, sole, sardines, monkfish, anchovies, pilchards

MEAT

chicken, turkey, turkey mince, lean red meat

VEGETABLES

peas, spinach, carrots, beetroot, potatoes, cabbage, broccoli, cauliflower, beans (French, runner, broad), sprouts, celery, celeriac, leeks, mushrooms, onions, sweetcorn, parsnips, turnips, swede, lettuce, watercress, peppers, cucumber

FRUIT

bananas, apples, pears, grapes, oranges, grapefruit, lemons, limes, pineapple, mango, lychees, guava, passion fruit, figs, dates, melon (Galia, watermelon, Cantaloup, Piel de Sapo), apricots, peaches, nectarines, raspberries, strawberries, blackberries, pomegranates, tomatoes

OTHER

bread (wholemeal, pitta), rice (wholegrain), pasta (wholemeal), cereals, nuts (almonds, walnuts, brazils, chestnuts), seeds (pumpkin, sunflower, sesame), herbs (dill, mint, parsley, basil), spices (ground tumeric, cumin, coriander, chilli), tomato purée, chopped tomatoes, eggs, lentils, baked beans, soya beans, red kidney beans, butter beans, skimmed or semi-skimmed milk, low-fat margarine, low-fat cottage cheese, low-fat yogurt, reduced-calorie mayonnaise, low-calorie sweetener, Lo-salt, low-calorie drinks, mineral water

TABLE 20

Fresh, rather than bottled herbs, are the best to use if they are available. If the quantity in which they are sold is too great for your needs, it is possible to freeze many herbs by chopping them up and putting them in an ice-cube tray topped up with water. When frozen, put the cubes in freezer bags and when you want to use the herbs, simply melt the ice, drain off the water and add the herbs to your food. It is also possible to grow your own herbs on a window-sill or in the garden.

When buying dried herbs and spices, go to a shop which has a fast turn-over and buy in small quantities as they quickly lose their freshness. They should always be stored in a dark place. Try buying whole spices and grinding them yourself with a pestle and mortar or coffee grinder – it is worth the effort for the aroma and taste.

WALKING MAKES YOU SLIM

You may be using the FITNESS WALKER'S DIET for a variety of reasons – to eat more healthily, to lose weight or to maintain your ideal weight – and dieting on its own is an inefficient way of doing this. We have already seen how only five per cent of people who calorie-count are successful in the long term. On the other hand, adopting a sensible balanced approach to food in the way suggested above is a far better way of losing and maintaining body weight, but this can only be successful if carried out as part of a total lifestyle approach to diet and exercise.

Dieting on its own is boring, negative and ineffective. But used with an exercise routine that is easy and achievable, it can shed excess weight and keep it off forever. Fitness walking is the easiest way to exercise regularly and to help lose 1–2 lb each week in the process. And it's the 1–2 lb weight-loss each week that can be kept up, as opposed to the yo-yo method of crash dieting.

It is by making small daily improvements in your diet, and walking regularly, that you can bring about the changes that will affect the rest of your life. No quick fixes; just consistency and persistence with a method that works.

Dieting without exercise actually slows down the metabolic rate, and then, when you stop dieting, the body puts weight on easily because it has become used to its slower way of working. In contrast, regular aerobic fitness walking increases the heart and respiratory rate, and speeds up the metabolism, helping to burn off calories – and keep them off. Walking briskly at 3.5–4 miles per hour, you will burn off around 200 calories every 30 minutes. Your raised metabolic rate will continue to burn up calories for several hours after you have finished exercising. And there is also evidence to suggest that this increased metabolic rate may become permanent.

WALKING – THE BEST HIP AND THIGH CONDITIONER

Fitness walking has the greatest effect around the hips and thighs where fat tends to accumulate. Walking briskly is a natural motion – your upper legs and hips stretch forwards and backwards with each stride that you take; and your hips and buttocks move from side to side as your legs swing forward.

This natural motion tightens up the muscles in your hips, thighs and buttocks, burning away unwanted fat and helping you get back to a trim and attractive shape. So your increased metabolic rate and the tightening effect on the muscles all add up to walking being a natural slimming process that helps you control and maintain body weight.

To walk to your ideal weight, a good idea is to use an item of favourite clothing to measure your progress; try a pair of old jeans that are too tight. Weigh yourself, measure your height and make a note of the figures – and then see how quickly you can fit comfortably back into them.

The Height/Weight Chart (see Table 21) will help you check your ideal weight. For each height there is an acceptable weight range covering small to large frames. If you are a woman, your goal weight should be nearer the lower figure; for men, depending on build, it should be towards the higher end of the scale.

Don't become obsessed with weight watching. Weigh yourself once a week, and try to get back into your chosen piece of clothing. By following THE FITNESS WAL-KER'S DIET the excess pounds will soon start to fall away, and you will feel and look fitter and slimmer without any calorie-counting.

You now have a goal to aim for. Go for it!

FOUR WEEKS FROM NOW

To lose the recommended 1–2 lb each week, you must combine the diet with the four-week WALKFIT pro-gramme in Chapter Four (this assumes that you have already

Height without shoes ft in	Small frame st lb	Medium frame st lb	Large frame st lb
HEIGHT/WEIGHT CHART			
WOMEN			
4 10	7 2	7 12	8 7
4 11	7 4	8 0	8 10
5 0	7 7	8 2	8 13
5 1	7 10	8 5	9 2
5 2	7 13	8 7	9 5
5 3	8 2	8 10	9 8
5 4	8 6	9 0	9 12
5 5	8 10	9 5	10 2
5 6	9 0	9 10	10 6
5 7	9 4	10 0	10 10
5 8	9 8	10 5	11 0
5 9	9 12	10 10	11 5
5 10	10 3	11 2	11 10
MEN			
5 3	8 10	9 4	10 0
5 4	8 13	9 7	10 3
5 5	9 2	9 10	10 6
5 6	9 6	10 0	10 10
5 7	9 10	10 4	11 1
5 8	10 0	10 8	11 5
5 9	10 4	10 12	11 9
5 10	10 8	11 2	11 13
5 11	10 12	11 6	12 4
6 0	11 2	11 10	12 8
6 1	11 6	12 0	12 13
6 2	11 10	12 5	13 4
6 3	12 0	12 10	13 9

TABLE 21

done the WALKPLAN warm-up programme in Chapter Three, if necessary). It's diet and exercise together that get rid of the excess pounds and keep them off forever. Exercise helps to speed up your metabolic rate, which means that you will be burning up all that unwanted fat quicker than if you were simply dieting – and it's easier, cheaper and more enjoyable.

Walking at any speed will help you lose weight, but you will lose weight faster by walking at a brisk aerobic pace of between 3.5–4 miles per hour. At speeds of 2–3 miles per hour you will lose around 140 calories every 30 minutes; but at 3.5–4 miles per hour you will be burning up around 200 calories every 30 minutes. And at this speed, walking at your target heart rate, you will be gaining cardiovascular fitness as well as losing weight. You don't have to start THE FITNESS WALKER'S DIET at the same time as the WALKFIT programme, but it makes sense to do so.

Remember to warm up before you start to walk, then begin with a 20-minute brisk walk around your chosen route. As you follow the WALKFIT programme, you will gradually increase the time of your walks to 45 minutes in the third and fourth weeks – and you will be losing around 300 calories each time you do so. At the end of the four weeks you will have lost around half a stone and you will be fitter, healthier and slimmer than you have been for years.

In the introduction to this book we told you about the success of *The Walking Diet* on the *Kenny Live* TV Show in Dublin. Remember what Jim Kemmy said about the diet: 'It's up to you basically.' And he should know – he lost 42 lb.

But whatever you set out to lose, THE FITNESS WALKER'S DIET will help you get there faster. If at the end of four weeks you still have excess pounds to shed, then repeat Week Four of the WALKFIT programme until you get back to your goal weight.

Here's to the new slimmer you – enjoy your walking.

CHAPTER SEVEN

WALKTALL
The Answer to Stress

Today I have grown taller from walking with the trees.
KARLE WILSON BAKER

Increased leisure time and reduced working hours for all have remained an empty promise for most people. The theory was that technology would free us all from the drudgery of long stressful working hours and leave us more time to spend with the family, on spare time activities and for recreation. In the '80s we heard about teleworking and telecommuting; in the scenario presented to us by the futurists, an age of leisure was to be ushered in by people working from home, by flexible job sharing, and by more considerate and caring management. But the crash of '87 reminded us all of the harsh realities of life at home and in the workplace.

A recent survey of international business people found that instead of working fewer hours, many people were working harder than ever and were suffering from stress as a consequence. The survey found that 75 per cent of respondents worked more than 45 hours per week, and more than 60 per cent worked more than one weekend per month. And as for spending more time with their families, 44 per cent said that they spent fewer than two hours a week looking after their children. The survey also found that 80 per cent of respondents said that they suffered from stress at least once a week, with nearly 50 per cent suffering from stress every day. Although problems at work are a major contributor to tension, anxiety and stress, other factors such as change, uncertainty and lack of exercise also add to the risk.

Surveys tell us that less than 20 per cent of people take regular beneficial exercise; other surveys tell us that many adults are now watching television up to 24 hours a week. As a nation we are underactive, underexercised and over-stimulated.

William Wordsworth spoke about 'the dreary inter-course of daily life'. That's the effect that stress has on us. It makes life look grey and tiresome. It diminishes us. Like gravity, which pulls objects towards the ground, stress has the effect of grinding us down until we can't take any more. It leaves us with no time simply to 'stand and stare'. Our lives lack balance, vitality and zest – we are out of control.

STRESS AND YOU

The causes of stress on modern man are very different from those affecting our forebears. There is not the regular threat of physical danger that there was for our food-hunting ances-tors. Life was simpler then; when they were attacked they would either run away or fight; if the body's response to stress was poor, they died. Life was all about the survival of the fittest.

Life is much more complex now and other causes of stress have replaced those dangers. It is difficult to define 'stress', but generally it is how we respond to the demands that life makes on us. These demands can range from problems at work, bereavement or divorce, to bad traffic conditions, crying children or disagreements with neighbours. And at times we are left with the feeling that we just can't cope.

Often we hide the emotions which are our natural

response to such problems – we don't want to be seen as 'inadequate' – but our feelings get bottled up and as a result we suffer from even more tension. Left unchecked, stress affects the way our body functions, and our general health is quickly affected. This in turn can lead to physical problems such as high blood pressure and ulcers – and to mental problems, even to mental illness.

Harley Street specialist Dr Malcolm Carruthers says that 'Stress is like an electrical load on the circuit. Some of us are on three amp fuses, some on 13 or even 30 amps. Our tolerance is partly hereditary, partly how we train ourselves.' We all react to stress in different ways.

Stress is often associated with people in high-pressure, demanding jobs – people who are trying to keep all the balls in the air while they try to manage their business, personal and social lives. Yet recent evidence contradicts this. A study of civil servants in London showed that death from a heart attack was three times higher among lower-grade employees – for example, messengers and clerks – than among higher-grade employees. It seems that a boring routine job does not provide the sense of fulfilment and self-esteem required for optimum job satisfaction, which is the key to reducing stress in the workplace.

Further research by Robert Karasek of the University of Southern California and Tores Theorell of Sweden's National Institute for Psychosocial Factors and Health divides occupations into four categories: active jobs, low-strain jobs, passive jobs and high-strain jobs. They found that those in active jobs who worked under pressure, used their own initiative and had some autonomy in their work, suffered less stress than those in passive jobs that demanded little in terms of skills or decision-making. Ironically, the high-strain jobs were those involving heavy pressure to perform, but providing little flexibility, sense of initiative or personal control, such as assembly-line workers and telephone operators.

It seems that it is the lack of control and involvement in decision-making that is a major factor in causing stress. And this applies not only to the work situation, but to the rest of our lives as well where we feel things are out of control and we cannot change them for the better.

STRESS AND LACK OF EXERCISE

The civilised man has built a coach but has lost the use of his feet.

RALPH WALDO EMERSON

Apart from the normal stressful situations caused by work and personal problems, a further stress factor that affects many people is lack of exercise. The modern sedentary person spends too much time sitting and not enough moving around and exercising. It is hardly any wonder since there are so many conveniences to make travel easy without having to use one's own feet. But our new sedentary condition is bad news for our health, our fitness and our state of mind.

Fitness walking is the easiest way to deal with tension, anxiety and stress. Tight muscles, tired brains, and bodies which lack vitality and stamina respond best when challenged by regular, vigorous exercise. Studies show that people who exercise regularly can cope better with the stresses and strains of life. Researchers at the University of Massachusetts Center for Health and Fitness found a 14 per cent average drop in anxiety levels after a brisk 40-minute walk.

In another behavioural study, two groups of students were tested with problems which were largely insoluble. They were told that the test was a good indicator of their likely performance in college. One group consisted of students who took regular exercise while the other group took no exercise. Both groups were then told of their weak performances in the test. The non-exercising students showed increased blood pressure, muscle tension and anxiety; but the exercising students showed no increase in blood pressure and lower muscle tension and anxiety. Exercise had given them the edge to be able to cope with stress.

MEETING THE DEMANDS OF STRESS

We cannot eliminate stress completely from our lives. As Dr Hans Selye says in his book *The Stress of Life*: 'Stress is part of life. It is a natural by-product of all our activities. There is no more justification for avoiding stress than for shunning food, exercise or love.' And Dr Chandra Patel of the Department of Community Medicine, University College, London, compares stress to tuning the strings of a musical instrument: 'Too loose and there's no tune, too tight and we snap.'

Stress, it seems, is vital to our lives. But there is bad stress and there is good stress. Bad stress produces anxiety, fear, overwork, insomnia, boredom and low self-esteem. Good stress affects us in challenging situations such as starting a new job or meeting new people. It is really a question of organising and controlling our lives to cope with the harmful effects of stress and, where possible, trying to neutralise them.

We have to learn to say no.

Learning to cope with stress is saying no to the conditions that cause the stress in the first place. You can't do everything yourself, and no one should expect you to. Try delegating at home or at work. And take the time to look objectively at your work, your ambitions, your relationships. No matter how busy you think you are, there is always time to take stock of your life and see where you are going. And there is no better tonic for doing this than fitness walking – and walking tall. Whether you are trying to change a difficult situation at work or you want to cope better with your life and its demands generally, aerobic fitness walking can be of great value. It not only reduces anxiety and tension but can also help to improve your ability to deal with anxiety-ridden situations. It is the best stress control and stress management system that there is.

Walking tall will help you take control of your life; walking tall will put enthusiasm and zest back into your life; walking tall will set you free.

WALKING TALL – WALKING FREE

What do you suppose will satisfy the soul, except to walk free and own no superior?

WALT WHITMAN

The essayist William Hazlitt was a great walker, and enthused about the way walking can lead to the feeling of freedom and liberty: 'The soul of a journey is liberty, perfect liberty to think, feel, do just as one pleases. We go on a journey chiefly to be free of all impediments and of all inconveniences – to leave ourselves behind.' He spoke of walking giving him 'a little breathing space'. And he talked about the effect that walking had upon him: 'Give me a clear blue sky over my head . . . a winding road before me . . . I laugh, I sing for joy.'

William Wordsworth walked. Samuel Taylor Coleridge, the poet who wrote the *Ancient Mariner*, walked. Shelley, Keats and De Quincey all walked. Balzac, Rousseau,

Nietzsche, Robert Louis Stevenson, Jane Austen and Charles Darwin were great walkers. Thoreau, Emerson, Abraham Lincoln and Albert Einstein walked. The French novelist Gustave Flaubert always took long walks before sitting down to write; he claimed that walking set his imagination free and helped him write such masterpieces as *Madame Bovary*. Throughout the centuries, poets, romantics, writers and philosophers have all been great walkers and have praised the virtues of walking. 'Walk tall, walk free, and look the world right in the eye,' says a popular song. That's what walkers have been doing for thousands of years − and that's what you can do now.

You don't have to be a poet or a philosopher to walk tall and gain the benefits of walking. They used to call it the 'daily constitutional' − now they call it fitness walking. But whatever you call it, it has the potential to get you away from 'the dreary intercourse of daily life' and open your heart and mind to the feeling of freedom and liberty. It helps you regain control of your life and put things in perspective.

Wordsworth's first major poem was *An Evening Walk*. And his friend Coleridge, who often tramped around the Lake District, spoke lovingly about walking when he said: 'Such blessing is there in perfect liberty.' Honoré de Balzac, the French writer, enthused about the physical and spiritual benefits of walking: 'This first taste of freedom, physically experienced through the leg muscles, brought an indescribable alleviation to my soul.' Walking has this ability to take us out of ourselves, to stretch us physically and spiritually. It really does make us feel as if we are walking tall, and it really does make us free.

ACTION ABSORBS ANXIETY

These enchantments are medicinal. They sober and heal us.
They are plain pleasures. Kindly and native to us.

RALPH WALDO EMERSON

The easiest, most effective aerobic exercise to help you defeat stress is fitness walking. It is cheap, it can be done anywhere at any time and its benefits are not only physical but also psychological. Emerson, the great American writer, knew only too well about the simple pleasures of walking and its ability to heal the body and mind. Like Wordsworth, he was a lover of the outdoors and found much of the inspiration for his famous essays whilst out walking.

The reason is simple. The human body is not built for sitting – be it in a chair, a car seat, or at an office desk – it is designed to move. There is a yogi saying: 'Movement is life'. Unless we wake up to the effects that our sedentary lives are having upon us and do something positive about them, then stress will be the logical outcome of our inaction. At the very least we are likely to suffer fatigue, irritability and psychological and emotional discomfort. Then come the stiff necks, stiff backs, headaches and numerous physical problems associated with inactivity, which often remain undiagnosed.

When we sit, our head and shoulders tend to pull the body forwards under the force of gravity, and this places undue strain on the muscles and spine. Instead of sitting with good posture, many of us sit hunched over our work, and it is the cumulative strain on our bodies that eventually causes the tension and stress that many of us suffer from. In contrast, when we walk we come into our natural inheritance: our bodies are designed to move; they are designed to function in a regular rhythmical way. As John Buchan says in *Scholar*

Gypsies: 'As a man's mind is richly advantaged, so also is his body. He loses the sickly humours, the lassitude, the dullness, which oppress all sedentary folk.'

Walking is the answer to stress. Walking frees the mind from the stresses and strains of the day. It releases tensions that build up, sometimes out of all proportion. Going for a walk is as good and probably even better than having a rest. Dr Hans Selye said that 'voluntary change of activity is as good as a rest'. So when you are feeling tense or anxious, get out of your home or office and walk the tensions away.

Walking recharges our batteries after tension and stress have drained them of power and energy. It is as natural as breathing, and it is the regular rhythmical action that drains away tension from our muscles and leaves us with a feeling of pleasant tiredness and a calm, clear mind. Walking works because, as we hit our natural stride, we become unconscious of our body and its movement – we are aware only of the rhythm. We are borne along in a total body-mind experience which makes us whole. Birds fly; fish swim; man walks.

WALKING CREATES PERSONAL SPACE

We all need time to ourselves; time we can call our own; time when we can collect our thoughts, think about the day and where we are going. When we can do this, we are in control of our life; when we can't do this, life, or other people, control us. The secret is to make time and get out and walk.

Do it first thing on a morning. Make the time – get up half an hour earlier if necessary. Even if you have only ten minutes, you will feel the effect of your body 'gearing up' for the day – improving your circulation and supplying more oxygen to lift your spirits.

Instead of taking a coffee break, or stopping to have a cigarette, get outside and walk for ten minutes. Your head, your heart and your lungs will thank you for it. You will get an instant lift and you won't suffer any of the ill effects or the over-stimulation caused by caffeine and nicotine.

Instead of sitting around at lunchtime, go for a brisk fitness walk. Tension and anxiety tend to build up during the day, leaving you tired and listless around noon, so get out and walk away these negative effects. And at the end of the working day, walk home if you live near enough. Or if you are catching a bus or train, then walk a few stops before getting on; or get off a few stops earlier and walk the rest of the way.

Walk in the evening, either before or after supper (don't, of course, do your main fitness walking directly after any meal). It has a calming effect on the mind as well as draining away muscular tension and the pressures of the day. And after a good evening walk you will be ready to retire to bed for a sound night's sleep.

Regular fitness walking leads to positive, purposeful walking. Positive walking is like positive thinking – you approach life and its problems with more energy and enthusiasm. And you become more successful as your confidence and self-esteem grow.

STRESS AND TOTAL RELAXATION

To reduce stress in your life, you need to relax. To relax, the easiest and most convenient way is to walk away the stress. But walking itself is only part of a total approach that you need to employ if you are going to enjoy any real continuing success.

Total fitness (involving fitness walking and the additional exercises in Chapter Five) and a total health approach using THE FITNESS WALKER'S DIET are the way to tackle stress and control it. Stress destroys essential vitamins and minerals and lowers the body's immune response. A balanced nutritious diet, containing plenty of the right foods, is as important as exercise in the fight against stress.

And don't forget the effects that too much alcohol, smoking and tranquillisers can have on an already over-stressed body. For many, they are props to get them through the day. Try and cut down on them all – indeed, give them up eventually – and substitute them with a regular fitness walk.

Walk tall every day of your life and you will never look back. Feel yourself stretching upwards as you walk. Feel the motion through your feet, legs and arms. Let yourself go and follow the flow. It's the most natural thing in the world. The world is your oyster. Nothing is ever going to get you down, or keep you down, again.

CHAPTER EIGHT

WALKTALK
Your Questions Answered

Walking is the best medicine.

HIPPOCRATES

Hippocrates offered the above advice to his patients 2,000 years ago. Since then people have been discovering for themselves the physical and mental benefits of walking and today fitness walking is endorsed by medical and health authorities as the exercise of the '90s that people of all ages can do.

We have already seen how walking works to build fitness, slimness and cardiovascular health, and helps with relaxation. Fitness walking may also help with a whole range of medical conditions from pregnancy to cardiac rehabilitation. We emphasise, however, that fitness walking may not be the prescribed remedy for all people, particularly those with a diagnosed medical problem, and that if you are in any doubt as to your ability to take part in this activity you should discuss it with your doctor first. In the meantime, however, here is a more detailed look at how fitness walking may help *you*.

Walking and Pregnancy

As the authors of *The Exercise Plus Pregnancy Program* advise: 'It is far better to begin exercising today than to undertake one of the most strenuous exercises of all – your labour and delivery – in an out-of-shape condition.' And Anne Kashiwa, a women's fitness expert, says, 'It's a good idea to exercise while you're pregnant, and walking allows you to do so in the safest possible way.'

Traditionally, pregnancy has been treated almost as an illness, with as much rest as possible being recommended, but there is now evidence to suggest that moderate exercise such as fitness walking can be beneficial to both the mother and child. And while a lot of medical attention is given to the health of pregnant women – monitoring the foetus, advice on nutrition, etc. – relatively few recommendations are made as far as exercise is concerned. It is best to improve your cardiovascular fitness before becoming pregnant. Many women who become pregnant may already follow a fitness programme; but for others who have not exercised regularly, pregnancy is a strong motive for seeking the benefits of a fitness routine for both mother and child.

In either case, a pregnant woman should consult her doctor before commencing or continuing a fitness walking programme – a programme of exercise is not suitable for all pregnant women. If possible, try to become involved in a supervised walking programme where you can be carefully monitored. And in any case, consult your doctor about how far into your pregnancy you should continue exercising. A mother-to-be should listen to her own body, using common sense as a guide. Never push yourself too hard – the Rating of Perceived Exertion (RPE) in Chapter Four is the best guide here – and just walk to feel better and maintain fitness. Strenuous exercise may decrease the blood's supply of oxygen to the developing foetus, causing premature births and miscarriages and so on, and it can cause an elevation in the pregnant woman's body temperature which may damage the developing nervous system of the foetus. So remember – consult your doctor before exercising – even walking.

For those who have had little previous exercise, a

target heart rate of 60 per cent of the maximum is sufficient to begin with, working up over a period of several weeks to 70 per cent. This is a safe level and should not be exceeded. Those who exercised regularly prior to pregnancy should not exercise any harder during pregnancy – again, a target heart rate of 70 per cent of the maximum is sufficient for conditioning. A mile or two daily is all that is needed to keep active and maintain fitness, while sedentary women should begin slowly at a pace of 2 miles per hour for 20 minutes.

Many women have found that walking makes them confident and positive about themselves and about their pregnancy. As well as avoiding an excessive increase in weight by walking, this exercise can help women to cope with everyday routine as easily as possible. Walking as a regular exercise during pregnancy can help to prevent high blood pressure; and since walking tones the body, backache, fatigue and other discomforts often suffered during this time can be reduced to a minimum. Anxiety and stress can be alleviated and, at a time when women often feel physically awkward, walking helps to make them feel good about themselves.

Fitness walking should be preceded and finished by a short warm-up and warm-down. However, joints soften during a woman's pregnancy so be very careful when attempting even the most gentle of stretches. Avoid brisk exercise in hot, humid weather and at all times drink plenty of water to avoid dehydration. Do not exercise for long periods of time and if any unusual symptoms occur, stop walking immediately and consult your doctor.

After the birth, a well-toned mother will be able to return to her usual activities much sooner. This is important in order to be able to look after the baby and also for the mother's self-esteem – feeling strong and healthy after childbirth is a benefit that is valued highly. During this time, fitness walking is an excellent form of exercise. Although you should check with your doctor first, generally speaking you can start walking, initially at a gentle pace, as soon as your body feels ready. And as your strength gradually increases, the intensity and duration of your walking can build up slowly too, so that you have more energy to cope with all the new demands on your time, and are better prepared to cope with the numerous new stresses in your life.

Walking and Premenstrual Syndrome (PMS)

PMS affects more than 90 per cent of fertile women at some time, and in some women it is so bad that their work and social relationships are seriously affected. Indeed, many women complain of the various physical and emotional symptoms of PMS – such as headaches, depression and extreme tiredness – for anything up to 14 days before menstruation.

There are many conflicting ideas on the cause and treatment of the symptoms of PMS and very often a woman may take drugs, when performing a simple activity such as fitness walking could provide the remedy she seeks. Fitness walking is effective in reducing anxiety and muscular tension, and it can relieve depression – the mind works better when the body is in motion. As fitness walking can be done at any time and anywhere, it is an excellent exercise for anyone suffering from PMS.

For further help with symptoms of tension, anxiety and stress, refer to Chapter Seven above.

Walking and Back Pain

That which is used develops; that which is not used wastes away.

HIPPOCRATES

Ninety-five per cent of people in Britain will suffer from back pain at some time in their lives. 'Oh, if only I could do something for my aching back' must be one of the most common medical complaints. Fitness walking can provide relief for many people suffering from this condition.

'Taking a walk regularly is one of the best things you can do for your back. It promotes muscular development, increases circulation, and speeds up the release of endorphins which provide a natural "high",' says Dr John Regan, a surgeon at The Texas Back Institute. He goes on to say that: 'Walking also lacks the jarring impact associated with many other forms of exercise.'

Yoga teaches us that old age comes with the stiffening of the backbone; and it is this stiffening that causes loss of flexibility in the back and joints, and also affects the roots of the spinal nerves, affecting other functions of the body – circulation, digestion and respiration. For the spine to be healthy it needs to be supple, and for this to happen it must have exercise otherwise it receives less blood than it needs – which means less nourishment. Waste products are not carried away; muscles and nerves are affected; tiredness and ill-health ensue. Fitness walking can provide the exercise needed to help keep the back and joints flexible.

Our sedentary lifestyles and bad posture can lead to lower-back pain, and sitting for long periods of time can cause a shortening of certain postural muscles. If you sit down for lengthy periods during the day, your body weight is unevenly distributed on to the lower back and hips. Indeed, people who spend a lot of time driving a car may suffer similar problems. So just as it is important to get up from a chair at regular intervals and go for a walk, so it is for drivers to stop regularly and get out and stretch their legs. On the other hand, many lower-back injuries are caused by jogging (where the feet strike the ground with 3–4 times body weight) and dance aerobics (where the feet strike the ground with 4–5 times body weight). Fitness walking provides an ideal programme of exercise which can be built up gradually to give mobility to the back. It will also help those who have suffered an injury to this area (remember that fitness walkers' feet only strike the ground with 1–1.5 times their body weight). And it will help those who have been inactive for a long time and wish to start up a moderate fitness programme.

Fitness walking strengthens the muscles in the pelvis and lower back. If you have problems in this area, you may actually feel better walking than sitting, as the forward movement of the body reduces the force of gravity on your back. Sitting and standing can both put more strain on the spine than walking. It is important to emphasise that to develop mobility in this area, a programme of fitness walking and stretching exercises is necessary. It is total fitness which strengthens the back muscles and helps to alleviate aches and pains.

If you have a serious back problem, consult your doctor before starting out on a fitness walking and exercise programme.

Walking and Varicose Veins

Varicose veins are a common complaint, affecting women more than men. And prolonged standing, being overweight and hormonal changes during the menopause can all play a part in their onset.

Medical treatment is needed for this condition, but regular fitness walking which provides vigorous and continuous exercise can help many people. This should be discussed with your doctor. In any event, do not begin a programme of vigorous walking if you have varicose veins and you are overweight. Take things step by step. Firstly, try to reach your ideal weight. Cut down your fat intake, particularly the saturated fats – see Chapter Six for a low-fat way of eating. If you have to sit in one place for a long time, flex your calf muscles as this helps the circulation – and try to sit with your legs raised regularly. As you reduce your weight, you can gradually increase your walking.

Walking and Osteoporosis

As we get older there is a gradual decrease in skeletal strength. The mineral content of the bones decreases and their texture becomes thinner. And because the bones are too porous and brittle, they are more likely to fracture. This condition is known as osteoporosis, and fitness walking may help you combat it.

Osteoporosis affects women more than men – one in four compared with one in 40. And it is more common among heavy smokers and drinkers. However, although it can affect women as early as in their 20s, it is particularly prevalent after the menopause because the decrease of the hormone oestrogen at that time means that their bodies are losing calcium.

Calcium and exercise are the keys to the prevention and treatment of osteoporosis. This should begin in childhood and continue throughout life, with a good calcium diet to nourish and maintain the bones and regular exercise to maintain a strong skeleton. Sources of calcium are milk and milk products, green, leafy vegetables, citrus fruits and shellfish. Eat plenty of these to ensure an adequate intake.

Increasing bone mass is the aim here. Physical activity, particularly weight-bearing exercise such as fitness walking, will help. Fitness walking is the easiest and safest form of exercise for people of all ages and studies show that just half an hour, four times a week, can help prevent osteoporosis.

Walking and Cigarette Smoking

WARNING – SMOKING CAN SERIOUSLY DAMAGE YOUR HEALTH

We have all seen the message yet, despite the warning, smoking kills over 100,000 people in the UK each year. Women smokers are three and a half times more likely to suffer cervical cancer than non-smokers, and their babies are usually 200g smaller than average at birth, and tend to remain underweight until early adulthood.

And smoking not only harms the person who smokes. Through passive smoking, it can also affect the health of family and colleagues.

Smoking cigarettes is the single most important cause of early death and preventable disease. You increase your likelihood of heart disease by three times, and of lung cancer by 30 times by smoking more than a packet of cigarettes daily. The answer is simple – don't smoke. Studies have shown that a year after giving it up the risk of a heart attack is reduced by 50 per cent, and after ten years is comparable to that of a non-smoker. Even for those who have suffered a heart attack already, the risk of having a second or fatal one can be reduced by half after only three years of quitting. And the benefits can be immediate.

One problem people often complain of when they give up smoking, though, is that they tend to put on weight because they eat more snacks. Fitness walking can be of great benefit as it can help in weight control. Also, going out for a brisk walk in the fresh air can help to take your mind off any craving you may have – for either a cigarette or a snack! Try saving the money you would have spent on smoking and reward yourself by using it to buy a good pair of walking shoes.

It has been seen from studies that people who are active and fit are not so likely to smoke as those who are sedentary and less fit. Although walking does not actually stop people from smoking, the regular routine of fitness walking can be applied as a positive habit to replace the negative habit of smoking.

In order to improve your general health, you must find the will-power to stop. Smoking causes feelings of fatigue because it impairs the delivery of oxygen to the cells of all the body's organs; it destroys vitamin C in the body, impairing the immune system; and it increases the amount of carbon monoxide in the bloodstream, leading to heart and lung disorders and cancer.

Get wise. Give up, or start cutting down today, and replace the lack of oxygen and the excess of carbon monoxide in your system with the life-enhancing aerobic benefits of vigorous fitness walking. Walk regularly for a month. Feel the oxygen surging through your body – and you'll never want to touch a cigarette again.

Fitness walking is a positive addiction.

Walking and High Blood Pressure

Regular aerobic fitness walking can help reduce high blood pressure – hypertension – by making the heart work more efficiently and by improving the circulation. The blood vessels become more elastic and the amount of oxygen delivered to the tissues increases. It has also been shown that blood pressure can be reduced by weight loss. Regular fitness walking combined with a low-fat, high-fibre diet (as suggested in Chapter Six) is an excellent form of weight control.

Another condition often associated with high blood pressure is stress which, as we have seen, can also be reduced by regular fitness walking. Although blood pressure returns to normal quite quickly in a healthy person, prolonged high blood pressure puts added strain on the heart and kidneys, and may lead to a stroke or coronary thrombosis.

As well as following a regular exercise programme of fitness walking and watching your weight, there are other ways in which you can help yourself to reduce high blood pressure:

- do not smoke
- decrease your intake of alcohol and caffeine
- and make sure your diet is low in salt, sugar and fat.

Walking and Cholesterol

Cholesterol, although a controversial subject, is in fact essential to life. It is present not only in the bloodstream but in all of the body's tissues. Most of the cholesterol in the bloodstream is made in the body, but some foods which we eat contain cholesterol (dietary cholesterol).

Cholesterol is transported in the blood by lipoproteins. There are two types of lipoprotein – high-density (HDLs) and low-density (LDLs). HDLs are sometimes called 'good' and LDLs 'bad' cholesterol. The higher your HDL level the lower the risk of heart disease.

According to exercise physiologist Dr Adrianne Hardman of the University of Loughborough: 'Regular walking can increase the levels of "good" cholesterol in the blood, reducing chances of a heart attack.' She claims that exercise is the best lifestyle change you can make to increase the HDLs.

You can also affect your total cholesterol level through your diet. Dietary cholesterol is only found in foods of animal origin – in meat, eggs and dairy products. As a diet high in cholesterol and saturated fat can increase your blood cholesterol level, it is essential to reduce your intake of cholesterol and saturated fats.

Stress can also affect your cholesterol levels. When you are stressed, sugar from the liver is released into the bloodstream to provide extra energy for the muscles, and there may well be an excessive release of cholesterol too. So try to avoid stress – and relax. Go for a fitness walk.

Walking and the Heart

Fitness walking as an aerobic exercise can help to lower the risk of coronary heart disease (CHD) as it has been shown that there is a link between vigorous physical exercise and a low incidence of heart failure. Indeed, a lack of vigorous activity can be as big a risk to your health as smoking or high blood pressure.

Studies show that regular, vigorous exercise like fitness walking may reduce the risk of a heart attack by half. The exercise must be current, as exercise earlier in life does not count. Former athletes who now lead a sedentary lifestyle can be as much at risk as those who have never been active.

It is very important to build up gradually with a fitness walking programme. The WALKPLAN and WALKFIT programmes are designed to ease you gently into regular exercise. And ease is what it's all about. Strenuous exercise can be fatal; so take it gently and listen to what your body is telling you. Your body always knows best.

Although regular, vigorous exercise can reduce the risk of developing CHD, it cannot provide immunity. So many other factors have to be considered. And another way in which you can help yourself is by having a healthy, balanced diet as suggested in Chapter Six.

Walking and Cardiac Rehabilitation

People who have suffered a heart attack can benefit from fitness walking. Although damaged heart muscle cells cannot regenerate, exercise can help to reduce the work of the remaining tissue, and patients who exercise tend to be more able to cope with their return to normal activities. Confidence is gained in being able to exercise safely, and this can help combat any feelings of depression following a heart attack.

Many people can hope to lead a reasonably normal life within a few months of a heart attack. However, this depends on the severity of the attack – and on the personality of the person concerned. It is most important that you build up the amount of your activity gradually, in order to increase your strength steadily.

One of the first forms of exercise may be to go for a gentle walk. Your exercise can then become steadily more strenuous until you can walk briskly. Remember – everybody's progress on the road back to health is different. Of course, you must listen to your body – don't overdo the exercise. And discuss your exercise programme with your doctor.

The best exercise is walking. Even people who have suffered a heart attack are usually able to take up exercise such as this fairly soon – but clearly this must be done with the doctor's blessing. Walking is the easiest and safest way of seeking a healthy heart and lungs.

Walking and Arthritis

Arthritis is an inflammatory disease of the joints. According to rheumatologists, many people suffering from arthritis are able to benefit from regular fitness walking, and as it strengthens the muscles and ligaments attached to the arthritic joints, some of the pain can be alleviated. It may also prevent some of the joint inflammation itself.

People with arthritis may also suffer from depression, which in turn can lead to lethargy. Fitness walking is a natural anti-depressant and promotes feelings of well-being.

Walking and Children's Fitness

Children are natural walkers but, like many people these days, they are becoming increasingly sedentary – and unfit. Studies show that some children watch as much as 24 hours of television a week – and a child who develops bad habits is likely to continue them as an adult. A sedentary child will probably grow into a sedentary adult.

Fitness walking is an ideal exercise for the whole family. Walking with your children will get them into a good habit which will last them for the rest of their lives. And as well as promoting good health and fitness, walking offers an opportunity to do something together as a family.

Walking and Self-Confidence

When you feel fit and healthy your self-confidence increases and you feel more able to cope with the demands made on you. If things get too much for you, you can simply walk away from them.

If you want to lose weight and you have already started fitness walking, you will soon feel ready to change your eating habits. Using THE FITNESS WALKER'S DIET, you will be able to get back to your ideal weight and your self-confidence will quickly return as the pounds fall away.

Time spent fitness walking means time taken off from the stresses of daily life. As a result, you will feel less anxious. Regular exercise can increase the levels of endorphins – naturally secreted hormones – that appear to work in the brain, increasing a sense of well-being. And this feeling of contentment in turn increases your self-confidence.

CHAPTER NINE

FASTFEET
Footnotes For Fitness Walkers

*When you have worn out your shoes, the strength of the shoe
leather has passed into the fibre of your body. I measure your
health by the number of shoes you have worn out.*

RALPH WALDO EMERSON

NATURAL SHOCK ABSORBERS

The human foot is built like a suspension bridge; with its 26
bones, 56 ligaments and 38 muscles, it is an engineer's delight.
The weight is evenly distributed across its length by the
arching bones (the metatarsals) from the heel bones to the
toes. And a thick pad of fat and fibrous tissue (the plantarfascia)
under the sole of the foot, running from the heel bone to the
metatarsals, protects the foot as it makes contact with the
ground, making the foot a perfect natural shock absorber.

The feet carry the entire weight of the body, holding
it upright and maintaining the body's balance during walking.
Balance in the body begins here, and a balanced body moving
through space develops a sense of harmony which leads to a
balanced mind. It is this sense of balance and perfect grace of
movement that makes walking the best exercise to combat
tension and stress.

Although walking is a low-impact, low-stress exercise,
it is still necessary to look after your feet. The average person
walks about four miles a day, mainly on hard surfaces, and

the feet take a pounding of over 1,000 tons. If care is not taken, this constant pounding can cause them trauma and injury.

Footcare means walking with a natural gait – with a heel-to-toe rocking motion and a balanced, rhythmic stride. It means wearing socks that prevent odour and bacteria building up, and that help prevent blisters and callouses. But above all it means wearing shoes that fit well, and give comfort and support.

THOSE SHOES WERE MADE FOR WALKING

In walking, just walk; above all, don't wobble.

YUN-MEN

Walking is the cheapest form of exercise, the only equipment needed being a pair of well-cushioned shoes that give proper heel and arch support. A good walking shoe will help keep your feet in good shape – and that will help keep the rest of you in good shape too.

According to researchers at the Center for Locomotion Studies at Penn State University in the USA, when we walk the heel of the foot supports 60 per cent of the body weight, as against the forefoot which supports 28 per cent. Since most walking injuries are to the heel and forefoot, it's important to ensure that a walking shoe has adequate cushioning and support in these areas.

A major contribution to our knowledge of what happens to the body when it walks has been made in recent years through the study of biomechanics – the science of biological systems in motion. Biomechanical tests confirm that the foot lands with 1–1.5 times the force of body weight in walking compared with 3–4 times body weight in jogging. They have also shown that most walkers land on the outside of their heels, rotating their weight on to the inside edge before rolling it forwards on to the ball of the foot. If you look at a pair of worn shoes you will see the excessive wear to one side of the heel. More than 90 per cent of people walk with this kind of outside-to-inside motion as the heel strikes the ground, and this tendency is known as 'pronation'. (The opposite is called 'supination', where the heel rolls from inside to out when it strikes the ground). Pronation acts as a natural braking mechanism, but too much of it can create a twisting motion which translates into potential ankle, knee and hip injuries. On top of this, the rear foot can tend to wobble when you walk, so to control excess pronation and rear-foot wobble, and to cushion impact as the foot hits the ground, it is necessary to wear a shoe which gives you the right support and cushioning.

When you go shopping for a new shoe, it's a good idea to do this later in the day, since your feet tend to swell slightly as the day wears on. Wear socks like the ones you will be walking in and try both shoes on to test for comfort and fit. Stand up and walk around the shop before making a final decision to buy.

A comfortable pair of shoes for fitness walking may either be a specialist shoe (a specially designed fitness walking shoe), or a suitable training shoe, preferably a 'cross trainer', which is designed for participation in a whole range of activities – including walking. Some people use running shoes for fitness walking. However, hiking boots and shoes designed for rough terrain are unlikely to be suitable for urban fitness walking on pavements. They will be cumbersome and can cause injuries such as shin splints. If you are not using a training shoe of the type described above, then wear a shoe made from a thick resilient material such as foam rubber or crêpe.

When you buy a fitness walking shoe, look for the following features:

WEIGHT – choose a lightweight design; wearing a shoe which is too heavy causes you extra work and is tiring.

UPPER CONSTRUCTION – this should be sturdy, providing good support and made from a breathable fabric, preferably leather or a design using leather and fabric or mesh. Leather provides flexibility and breathability and gives good protection from the weather.

FIRM HEEL COUNTER – this is the cup at the back of the inside of the shoe; it wraps around the heel and helps to control excess pronation and rear-foot wobble. A good heel counter provides stability for the entire foot and leg; it should be firm, cushioned and reinforced, but not over-padded.

ROOMY TOE-BOX – this should allow the toes room to spread out when they hit the ground and during push off. Toes should be able to move easily up and down and back and forth, and should not feel too tight against any part of the shoe. The 'thumbnail rule' is a good guide when selecting a suitable walking shoe. To ensure the right shoe length, there should be a space the width of your thumbnail between the end of the toe-box and the tip of the longest toe on your longer foot.

CUSHIONING – the midsole (between the insole and the bottom of the shoe) is one of the most important areas for cushioning. EVA (ethyl vinyl acetate) is a lightweight material often used for extra cushioning here, and some shoes incorporate a new shock absorbing material called Hexalite.

Many shoes now include a removable cushioned insole which can be replaced when it breaks down.

OUTERSOLE – this is the bottom of the shoe that touches the ground. It should provide durability and should be shock-absorbent to protect your feet from bruising. The normal walking motion is to land on your heels and roll your weight forwards with a natural rocker motion on to your toes. Some shoes have a rocker profile sole to assist this natural heel-toe motion.

NOTCHED HEEL – this is the padded collar at the back of the shoe in the shape of a notch or a dip. It cradles the Achilles tendon and prevents pressure being put on it.

THE SOCK QUESTION

Good quality walking socks are a must; after a good walking shoe, they are the next most important consideration for foot comfort. But what type of socks, and one pair or two?

Although some people walk without socks, serious fitness walking should not be done without them. Not only do they protect the feet from injury, but they help to disperse perspiration which would otherwise eat into the lining of the shoes causing damage. The shoes can then become uncomfortable and may cause corns and blisters.

Feet can sweat as much as a cup of perspiration a day –

or half a gallon per foot per week – so it's necessary to wear absorbent socks that protect your feet and your shoes. The best socks are made of cotton or a blend of cotton and Orlon. These materials 'wick' away moisture, drawing perspiration away from your feet to leave them relatively dry and fresh smelling.

Some synthetic materials can do the opposite, leaving them hot, sticky and smelly. This moist environment within your shoes can then become a breeding ground for micro-organisms which can cause athlete's foot and other fungal infections.

Other socks which are suitable for walking include those made of wool, and blends of nylon with either cotton or wool. One type of branded sock available is made from an acrylic and nylon mixture and promises 'protection plus extra durability'. It has high-density padding at the ball and heel for extra protection against abrasion and blisters; low-density pads to protect the toes and cushion the instep against lace pressure; and another low-density pad for better arch support. Your best bet is to experiment until you find a sock that you are happy with.

As to whether you should wear one sock or two – opinion is divided. Some people suggest wearing two pairs: a thin inner pair of cotton to prevent chaffing, and a thicker outer pair to cushion the feet, keep them warm and absorb sweat. Certainly, in the winter it is a good idea to wear two pairs to keep out the cold, but it really is a question of experimenting to find the best solution for yourself.

It goes without saying that socks should be a good fit. When you are walking at about 1,400 to 1,800 steps per mile, it only takes a slight rubbing each step to cause a blister.

Finally, change your socks every day; and if you perspire a lot, change your socks whenever they get wet.

Fungus thrives in a warm, sweaty environment and if you are not careful this can lead to infections. Never wear socks twice in a row without washing them. If they are only sweaty, not dirty, they can be washed out in the sink by hand very quickly and drip-dried. It's worth the effort if you want to enjoy the comfort of troublefree walking.

FOOTFAULTS – KNOW THY FEET

According to the leading British footcare company, Scholl, two out of three people suffer from foot problems, and shoe fit is recognised as the key influence in these problems. It goes without saying that preventive footcare in the form of well-fitting, comfortable shoes is the best way to look after your feet.

Care of the feet is very important. We depend on them every day to transport us around, but it seems that we take little notice of them until they begin to ache. Tired, aching feet and hot feet are the most common foot problems, but from time to time you may suffer from one of the following:

Corns and Callouses

Corns and callouses are the result of pressure and friction on the feet caused by badly-fitting shoes. Corns can be hard or soft, the hard ones usually appearing on the little toe and the soft ones between the toes. The skin thickens and a core of dead skin develops, thus producing a corn. Callouses, which are areas of hard skin, may appear on the toes, the balls of the feet or on the heels.

Corns and callouses can be treated by soaking the foot

in warm water and gently applying a pumice stone or foot file. You may have to follow this procedure a few times – be careful not to rub too hard as it will make the skin raw. Afterwards, protect the area with a light pad.

Blisters

Blisters are also caused by friction – between the feet and badly-fitting shoes or socks. They are formed by the layers of skin cells separating and filling with fluid; and often occur during hot weather, when the feet sweat and swell, or if shoes and sandals are worn without socks or stockings.

A small blister can be left to heal naturally, but you can cleanse the area, being careful not to break the blister, and cover it with a thin pad with a hole in the middle for light protection. Large blisters and any which break should be cleansed and covered with a light bandage, but do watch for any sign of infection, in which case you should seek professional advice.

Athlete's Foot

This fungal infection usually occurs between the toes, particularly the outer toes, but it can also affect the toe nails. There may be red scaling and tiny blisters and the affected area may become itchy.

There are several creams and powders available for this condition. However, try to prevent it by keeping your feet clean and dry. Always dry thoroughly between the toes, and wear dry socks or stockings, clean on every day, and well-ventilated shoes, alternating pairs so that they have a chance to air.

Bunions

Bunions are not only disfiguring but also painful. They are caused by the large metatarsal bone angling outwards at the big toe joint which forces the toe itself inwards. The pressure over this distended joint causes swelling and eventually a bunion forms. Professional advice should be sought as, if neglected, a bunion can affect standing and walking.

Flat-footed people are more likely to be affected by bunions, and a tendency to bunions may be hereditary although they can also be caused by badly fitting shoes. Women are more prone to them than men so it is advisable to wear shoes with a low heel and with ample width for the toes.

Badly fitting shoes are almost always to blame for the deformity of the toe bones, usually of the second, third or fourth toes, known as hammer-toes. Corrective pads can help but, most importantly, shoes that fit well should be worn. Professional advice should be sought if the condition proves painful or affects walking.

In-growing Toe Nails

This condition usually affects the big toe. The side of the nail cuts into the soft toe tissue which causes redness and swelling. In-growing toe nails can be extremely painful and can cause infection. They can be the result of tight fitting shoes but they can also be caused by cutting the toe nail badly. The nail should always be cut straight across, preferably after a bath when the foot has been soaked in warm water.

If you have an in-growing toe nail, put some strands of absorbent cotton under the nail, after soaking the foot in warm water, to prevent the nail from digging into the skin.

However, if there is swelling or the condition is very painful, seek professional advice.

Walker's Heel

This name is sometimes used for heel problems, including bone bruising. As we grow older, the pads of fatty tissue on the heel become thinner and, with repeated pressure on the bone and muscles here, pain can set in.

Inflammation of the joint, nerve and tendon can also cause pain in this area. These conditions – arthritis, neuritis and tendinitis respectively – must be treated medically. For bone bruising, the best treatment may simply be rest, thus taking pressure off the heel, although heel pads can be inserted into the shoes to act as shock absorbers.

Achilles Tendon

The Achilles tendon is the thick tendon at the back of the leg connecting the foot and heel to the calf muscles. A complete or partial rupture here is not usual for most walkers, but they may suffer from inflammation of the Achilles tendon. This can be caused by inadequate walking shoes or by a sudden change of routine – wearing a different type of shoe or walking on a different surface. It is a painful condition and stiffness and swelling can occur. (It can be seen how important stretching exercises are before walking as they limber up the tendons ready for the exercise to follow.)

If you injure the Achilles tendon, avoid over-stretching. Walk at a moderate pace and only on flat surfaces. Applying ice or cold water may help reduce the pain. And make sure you are getting the correct support from your shoes.

FURTHER FAULTS FOR FITNESS WALKERS

Shin Splints

Shin splints are a pain in the front of the shin. Though damage or splintering of the shin bone itself is suggested by its name, the pain can be caused by several other conditions, such as inflammation of the tendon attached to the bone of the lower leg, irritation of the membrane between the bones of the lower leg, a muscle imbalance or a muscle spasm occurring due to a swelling of the muscle.

The pain will be felt in the lower leg when weight is put on the foot and the shin may be tender when touched. Again, a good choice of shoe is essential in order to avoid this, and walking on grass offers a softer surface than walking on the pavement.

Strains and Sprains

A strain is the stretching or tearing of a muscle or tendon whereas a sprain is the stretching or tearing of a ligament. Blood vessels break leading to a swelling in the surrounding tissue as a result of which there may be pain and bruising in the area affected.

The most common problems when walking, particularly on rough ground, are strains and sprains of the ankle. If a sprain is slight, a short rest will probably be all that is required, but if it is bad, it is essential to rest the leg. Putting the foot into cold water helps to stop the bleeding and the ankle should be bandaged firmly. Professional help should be sought as there could be problems later if the ankle is not treated properly.

The Knee

The knee is the largest and most complicated of the body's 187 joints. It is also the most vulnerable and the most frequently injured. It is a true hinge joint, the two main bones being the thigh and shin bone to which are attached all the leg muscles and ligaments which are necessary for the efficient support and movement of the joint.

The most common serious injuries to the knee involve tears of the ligament and problems with cartilages which pad and lubricate the joint. But generally knee pains are to do with the knee-cap. At times the knee-cap does not move smoothly against the thigh bone and as a result there may be swelling and pain. Alternatively, the knee-cap sometimes moves from side to side with every step. It is thought that such problems may be caused and aggravated by the way in which the foot hits the ground so it is important to try different walking methods. In spite of its vulnerability, though, the knee can withstand quite a large degree of stress.

Walking is an extremely good form of exercise for people who have had knee injuries as it is a low-impact activity which puts minimal stress on the joints. Walkers are therefore not as likely to experience the injuries or the prolongation of the injuries suffered by people who go in for high-impact exercise like jogging. If, however, you have a problem with your knees it is a good idea to avoid walking on hilly or rough ground and stay on flat, grassy surfaces. Of course, if you have had a serious knee injury it is necessary to discuss any exercise programme with a physiotherapist or doctor. But walking more than any other form of exercise may be just what the doctor ordered!

Muscle Cramps

A muscle contraction, causing cramp, can happen during activity or when resting. Although occasionally you may feel the onset of cramp, it usually occurs without any warning and it can be very painful. Causes of muscle cramp range from cold and tiredness to unconditioned muscles being over-stretched. You can generally stop it by stretching and pummelling the muscle. But it is advisable to reduce the likelihood of muscle cramps by doing warming up and cooling down exercises at either end of any vigorous activity.

Hopefully, if you take care of your feet, particularly when buying shoes, you should not suffer from any of these foot problems. Remember, if you look after your feet, they will look after you.

CHAPTER TEN

INNER WALKING
How to Be your Own Best Friend

The cure of the part should not be attempted without treatment of the whole. No attempt should be made to cure the body without the soul.

PLATO, *The Republic*, 382 BC

Inner walking is an invitation to explore yourself, to deepen your understanding of yourself – the real self which is waiting to be discovered beneath the mask which is your everyday self. It is an invitation to be your own best friend.

Remember when you were eight years old and the sky was the limit? When the sky really was blue every day, the world full of fairy-tale princesses, handsome princes and anything seemed possible. But then something happened – you grew up.

And you had to conform: at school, at work, in your everyday life. And your dreams dissolved as the harsh reality of earning a living and making your way in the world took over. You lost some of your sense of wonder and life lost some of its fizz.

Yet, despite some of the loss, you still experience times when you can make contact with your dreams and the deeper reality which is your real self – your centre, your authentic self, who you really are. Odd moments of reverie, day-dreaming, times when you can just 'let things happen': weekends, holidays, times when you can make some personal space for yourself.

The problem is that for many of us there are not enough of these experiences to make any real difference to our lives and spur us into action. For brief moments we have a vision of what we could be like; for brief moments we discover again the child within, trying to break out and express itself; for brief moments we become our own best friend. And all we had to do was ... but ... if only ... and then life comes crowding back in upon us again with its incessant round of 'getting and spending', as the poet Wordsworth called it.

What we need is a way of getting back in touch with our 'inner child', 'our best friend', without having to wait for our busy lives to make time for us. We have to make the time ourselves. We have to set aside the time to get back in touch with ourselves.

Some people use yoga, prayer, meditation and other inner disciplines to get back in touch with themselves and the deeper reality within. We now want you to try another method which works for us, and we feel sure will work for you if you give it a try. And that is inner walking.

Although walking can improve the condition of your heart, help you control your weight and improve your general fitness, many walkers may not realise that inner walking can actually change their attitude to life itself.

Inner walking combines the benefits of aerobic exercise with the meditative tradition of the East, where spiritual and psychological health is valued as highly as physical health, where the body and soul are treated as a whole, and where self-knowledge is prized above all.

Fitness walking stretches our bodies; inner walking stretches our minds and our souls. The secret of inner walking consists of knowing how to walk, how to breathe, and how to smile at ourselves – for we take ourselves far too seriously. Tension, anxiety, stress, depression, insomnia, and the thousand and one problems that cause physical and mental trauma are all symptoms warning us that we are out of balance. Inner walking restores that balance – helps us find something that we have lost, or perhaps forgotten. Inner walking helps us smile at ourselves, and at everybody we meet along the way. Inner walking sets free the creative force within; helps us rediscover our 'inner child' and our 'best friend'. Inner walking makes us whole.

FITNESS OF THE SPIRIT

I took a walk. Suddenly I stood still, filled with the realisation that I had no body or mind. All I could see was one great illuminating Whole.

HAN–SHAN, 16th-century Zen master

The walker Hal Borland echoed the Zen master when he said: 'All walking is discovery. On foot we take the time to see things whole.' The search for wholeness is the goal of inner walking. We walk to discover 'our better self', the self that puts us back in touch with our deepest reality. Indeed, even in the 19th century, in the midst of the Industrial Revolution, with its mass migration of people away from the land to the city, Wordsworth was able to express his concern about our loss of 'self': 'when from our better selves we have too long been parted by the hurrying world'. And in modern times, the walker-writer H. I. Brock has suggested that walking can help regain this loss of self: 'The land of our better selves is most surely reached by walking.'

When we talk about 'the meaning of life', 'the inner

161

person,' or 'enlightenment', we are seeking our better selves. And the way to do that is to get away from the hurly burly of the day, relax and still the mind. And the easiest way to do this is to walk.

When you try to sort out your problems with thought alone, when you try to discover meaning and a deeper understanding of life with thought alone, then you become stuck in the workings of the conscious mind – your day-to-day mind, the mind that is causing you all the problems in the first place. If you use your mind to work on your mind, you will end up more confused than when you began. You get caught up in a mental experience; the mind is muddied with 'interference' and 'brain noise'. And in this kind of disturbed state, it is impossible to see clearly and to see things whole.

The answer is to get outside of your mind, cut the noise out of your system; and the way to do this is to move your body; to make your body and your spirit fit; and the easiest way to do this is to walk.

Fitness of the spirit energises us. As we pay attention to the movement of the body, removing from our mind all the clutter of chaotic thoughts, suddenly the mind relaxes and clears. Think of the effect a stone has if you throw it into a pool. The stone hits the water, causing waves of interference, then gradually the waves subside and the pool clears again. Your mind is like that pool much of the time, with sensory events bombarding it from morning to night – noise, crowds, traffic, telephones, televisions, videos and a thousand anonymous forms of mind pollution. But when you walk – when you use inner walking and walking meditation to still the mind – then you suddenly become aware, let go of all the clutter which is filling up your thoughts, and you see things whole.

Meditation and awareness begin with the body. 'Sit

as little as possible,' wrote the philosopher Nietzsche. 'Give no credence to any thought that was not born outdoors while one moved about freely – in which the muscles are not celebrating a feast too.' Inner walking helps you do this. Inner walking is a total experience. You were born to move – your body, your heart, your mind and your spirit (or your soul, if you prefer). Moving the body and spirit; this is what recreation really means – re-creation, putting you back together; making you whole.

As you walk and your body 'feels' the rhythm, 'becomes' the rhythm, you will find that you become involved in a process, a flow, like a river and it's this flow experience – the flow of breath, the flow of the body, the flow of air around you – that slows and stills the mind and spirit. Inner walking invites us to be, to become, the real, authentic, 'better selves' that we really are.

THE FLOW EXPERIENCE

How can a man's life keep its course if he will not let it flow?
How can I become still? By flowing with the stream.

LAO TSE

Inner walking is a dynamic process. It energises us; awakens us; and stills our mind. We begin to experience what can only be called 'the walker's high'. When you have been walking for a time and you fully relax, your mood can change and give you a physical and spiritual uplift. Some people think that this is because the body releases powerful brain chemicals called endorphins into the bloodstream. But we feel that it is more to do with a change of perception, from the everyday conscious mind into 'the higher mind' – the intuitive mind: our better self.

As we walk, everything begins to slow down (except us, that is). The world at around four miles an hour looks a different place. Away from the stresses and strains of the day, we regain our senses. And as we listen to our own silent rhythm, to the sacred drum – the pulse of life itself, our own heart beating – we become one with the basic rhythm of the universe; the ebb and flow of the oceans, the daily motions of the planets, the movement of the seasons.

We become whole. And you too will find your better self when you open your mind to inner walking.

THE INNER GAME OF WALKING

Every path, every street in the world is your walking meditation path.

THICH NHAT HANH

Inner walking is a game: an inner game that you need to learn and practise. It's a new way of looking at things, seeing things in a different way – a different light. And it's learning how to listen. Hermann Hesse expresses the feeling in the treasured classic *Siddhartha*: '... how to listen, to listen with a still heart, with a waiting open soul, without passion, without desire, without judgement, without opinions'.

Inner walking is WM – walking meditation. Like traditional methods of meditation it goes beyond linear thinking and helps you find creative solutions to problems. It puts you back in touch with your better self, and shows you how to get back in touch whenever you want to. It is strong medicine: stronger than alcohol, drugs and tranquillisers. Yet it is a positive addiction, gentle, harmless and freely available to everyone. As Alan Watts, philosopher, mystic and advocate of walking meditation says:

Let your ears hear whatever they want to hear; let your eyes see whatever they want to see; let your mind think whatever it wants to think; let your lungs breathe in their own rhythm.

When we talk about WM, we don't mean thinking about our problems; that is thought. WM is a process, a flow experience, the letting go of conscious thought. WM shows you how to handle what's going on in your head. You become aware of the clutter, the 'brain noise', the confusion, the never-ending 'inner newsreel' of daily events. WM lets things just happen. It doesn't force events. It helps you let go; helps you wait and listen.

WM helps you collect information about yourself: how you feel; how you react to distance, speed, your surroundings, the seasons. There are few times when we are really with ourselves. WM allows just that; to be more receptive and aware; to focus on the here and now – to surrender to the intensity of the moment.

The practice of meditation is a mind-body process, and the purpose of walking meditation is mindful awareness – noticing your movements as you walk; being aware of the process – and concentration: counting footsteps, counting breaths to help you still the undisciplined mind. As the Indian classic, the *Bhagavad-Gita*, advises: 'Patiently, little by little, a man must free himself from all mental distractions.' It is by concentrating on 'one point' – on one thing at a time – that the mind is stilled and centred. Then energy, vitality and creativity flow out of it like the rays of the sun.

Start WM the way you started fitness walking – slowly, doing a little at a time. Don't push yourself too quickly. Get into your stride, build up a walking rhythm, and then experiment with different inner walking techniques. Start with five minutes of WM, and increase gradually over a few weeks to 15 or 20 minutes.

The following are all methods that you can use as walking meditational techniques. Try them; experiment with them.

Movement Meditation

The purpose of this meditation is to concentrate on your body movement and the rhythm of walking. To function at their best, the mind and the body need regularity, and rhythmic walking is the easiest way to achieve this.

There is a creative force and power that exists in rhythm. All nature has rhythm in it: the earth, sun and moon all move with a definite rhythm. To be successful, music must have rhythm. When we have rhythm in our movement, we become stronger and fitter, physically and spiritually. Indeed, Jean Jacques Rousseau had this to say about the rhythm of walking: 'I can only meditate when I am walking. When I stop I cease to think; my mind only works with my legs.'

WM creates this sense of rhythm when we walk mindfully and become aware of our movement. Feel the spring of your heel and toes as they make contact with the ground and propel you forward. Experience the pull of muscles in the feet, legs and hips. Note the rhythm of your arms, the movement of your head. Then stay with these feelings and get to know them.

Focus your attention on the relationship between your strides and your breathing. Note that this also is rhythmic, and that as you change your strides, so your balance moves and changes also.

As you continue with movement meditation, walking

will be experienced more as a process and a flow than simply a space between two points.

Oliver Wendell Holmes in *The Autocrat of the Breakfast Table* had the following to say about the mental pleasures of walking:

> The pleasure of exercise is due first to a purely physical impression, and secondly to a sense of power in action. The first source of pleasure varies of course with our condition and the state of surrounding circumstances; the second with the amount and kind of power, and the extent and kind of action. In all forms of active exercise there are three powers simultaneously in action, – the will, the muscles and the intellect. Each of these predominates in different kinds of exercise. In walking, the will and muscles are so accustomed to work together and perform their task with so little expenditure of force, that the intellect is left comparatively free. The mental pleasure in walking, as such, is in the sense of power over all our moving machinery.

Counting Breaths

This is easy to do. As you walk, count your exhalations up to four and begin again. If you lose track – because you think of something else – then bring your mind gently back to the task, and continue counting. You don't have to stick with counting up to four – in Zen the usual practice is to count up to ten.

Remember that the air we breathe is the very essence of life. Counting breaths is a way of getting back in touch with the basic rhythm of life; the inhaling and exhaling of our lungs is like the ebb and flow of the oceans and the movement of the planets.

The purpose of counting breaths is to concentrate on

one point. Don't be put off this task when other thoughts intrude and you start thinking about what you are going to eat later or what you are going to watch on television. Simply bring the mind gently back to counting breaths.

Another method is to pick out a lamp-post or a tree a few hundred yards along the road and count your breaths until you get there. This will help you to anchor your mind and focus awareness. After a few weeks you will experience increased concentration, awareness, and you will have mastered a simple way of stilling the mind.

Counting Footsteps

This is another simple method to develop awareness. You can count up to ten, 20, or 100, either forwards or backwards, repeating it over and over. When you have tried this method, then try the following method:

1. Count your first seven steps.
2. With your next step, begin at one and count to eight.
3. Then with your next step, begin at one and count to nine.
4. Continue in the same way until you reach 12.
5. Repeat the sequence from the beginning as many times as you like.

Repeating a Mantra

A mantra is a word or phrase that you repeat over and over again to focus your awareness. It is one of the most widely used forms of meditation in mystical training schools. The purpose again is to be doing just one thing at a time.

The word or phrase that you choose can either be something with special meaning to you, such as 'peace' or 'peace to all', or simply an abstract word or phrase – 'iam' or 'iam-eeh'. As you walk, repeat your mantra over and over. Immerse yourself in its sound. Feel the rhythm of the mantra as you continue chanting it. And stay with it, bringing your mind gently back to the task if it begins to wander.

Pleasure Meditation

John Hillaby, England's greatest walker, who has travelled over 200,000 miles and has written extensively on the pleasures of walking, says that he has got into the practice of intoning aloud, 'as a priest might do'. As a walker and a naturalist, he likes to remind himself of the different types of grasses if he is walking in the country. When he is walking in towns and cities, he observes the architecture and is able to tell the different types of brick that buildings are constructed of. He says: 'I always try to keep my mind alive ... When you are walking well ... it is not only a matter of aesthetics, but also of eurythmics, from the Greek word *eu*, which means good.'

The writer J. B. Priestley has also affectionately described the pleasures of walking and talked about the 'skull cinema', by which he meant the meditational effects brought about by the simple process of putting one foot in front of the other.

Pleasure meditation is simply meditating entirely for your personal pleasure. Unlike other meditations, there are no goals, or problem solving disciplines involved. Just walk for the pleasure of it. Create your own 'skull cinema', and think of your own ways of developing pleasurable awareness.

Just watch yourself as you walk; observe the process – the changing sensations, feelings, thoughts. Inner walking is the mediator between the life of the senses and the life of the spirit.

The Thinking Walk

Many of the world's greatest thinkers have walked to do their thinking. *Ambulando cogitans* or *ambulando solvitur* are commonly used Latin tags to describe the effects of walking on the mind. Quite simply, they mean that walking is good for cogitation and problem-solving.

Freud and Beethoven walked through Vienna and Einstein walked around Princeton. All of these men used the thinking walk to 'tap' their imaginations and free the intuitive mind. Pure thinking alone is not enough for true creative activity – eventually the mind becomes tired, exhausted and goes to sleep.

It takes the thinking walk to give us the feeling of being wide awake, and to shake us into action. Its swinging, rhythmic action unites the conscious and unconscious mind in a way that thinking alone can never do.

The Non-Thinking Walk

The purpose of this walk is to walk without thinking; simply to let the unconscious mind take over and sort out a particular problem. Try it for yourself. Before your walk, go over in your mind the problem to be solved – then forget about it. Don't try and force a solution; let it germinate in the mind in its own good time.

Relax. The problem solving process goes on without your conscious interference. Suddenly, the answer will appear to you in the most unexpected way. It may be during the walk, the next walk that you take, or even days later.

This sort of meditation is of the Zen type: to think without thinking. It opens new pathways in the mind that take you closer to your deeper and 'better' self.

Watching Your Thoughts

The purpose here is to clear your mind so that it becomes a blank space. As you walk, just observe the thoughts that come into your mind, note them, and then clear your mind again. Begin again and repeat the process. Don't make any judgements – just observe; pay attention. Watching your thoughts in this way will give you an insight into your attitudes and the way your mind works.

INNER WALKING AND CREATIVITY

Don't go outside yourself, return into yourself.
SAINT AUGUSTINE

What we want to know is who we are; how we can be happy; how we can make a success out of our lives. And what we are really trying to do much of the time in all our mad, confused, chaotic ways is to separate the prose from the passion that we so desperately need. Our lives are prosaic and humdrum enough; we need more passion, enthusiasm and love to make it all worthwhile. We need something to take us out of ourselves, so that we can be the 'better selves' that we know we can be. We need a 'lift'.

On the road, you get that lift – walking meditation gives you that lift. On the road you find answers to the great questions of life. WM opens the mind to the mystery of life; and opens the heart to the mystery of itself – the god within. This is what enthusiasm literally means: *entheos* (Greek for 'the god within').

171

WM is a creative way of distracting the conscious mind from its everyday routine and opening it up to the energy and power of the 'higher mind' – the 'intuitive mind'. This is the lift that you need – what the psychologist Abraham Maslow refers to as a 'peak experience':

> They tend to change a person's view of himself in a healthy direction ... they may change his view of other people and his relationships with them. They can change more or less permanently his view of the world ... they can release greater creativity, spontaneity, expressiveness, idiosyncracy.

Others put it differently:

> One's eyes are suddenly opened; oneself and the world appear in a different light, are seen from a different viewpoint ... the process can be described as a series of ever widening experiences which are felt deeply and which transcend theoretical, intellectual knowledge.
>
> *Erich Fromm*

> A man should learn to detach and watch that gleam of light which flashes across his mind from within ... yet he dismisses without notice his thought because it is his. In every work of genius we recognise our own rejected thoughts.
>
> *Ralph Waldo Emerson*

> I can remember the very spot in the road, when to my joy the solution occurred to me.
>
> *Charles Darwin*

Peak experiences shake us awake; summon up meaning; and open us up to the magnificent possibilities that we have as human beings. Our eyes are opened, and we see the world in a different light. The poet, the musician and the philosopher have always known this, and it is why they are able to create

172

works of genius. Your peak experiences may not urge you to create works of genius, but in your own special way they will help you to become a better person – a 'better self'.

KEEPING AN INNER WALKING DIARY

Only the man who can relax is able to create and ideas reach his mind like lightning.

CICERO

Walking meditation will help you relax, give you power over your mind, and open up the pathways to your 'better self'. If you practice WM regularly, you will soon be able to make contact at will with your intuitive mind and the 'peak experiences' that it generates. And you can then use these creative insights to improve your life, your work, and your relationships.

Generating intuitive insights is one thing; remembering them is another. There is nothing more infuriating than walking along and being shaken away by an 'intuitive flash', only to find that a moment later the experience has dropped out of your mind as quickly as it entered – and it cannot be recalled.

The answer to this is to keep an inner walking diary. Jot down experiences as they happen, then write them up later when you have the time. Keeping a diary helps keep you motivated and gives you the satisfaction of observing the progress you have made. Your peak experiences are discoveries to be recorded and treasured.

Write them down, and after a few weeks look through your jottings to see if there is any sort of pattern in them. You may find that from the fragments that spring up during walking meditation, a pattern does begin to emerge. Make a poem out of the fragments, or a word collage. Try word association games and see where the patterns take you. You will be surprised where your intuitive insights will lead you. Suddenly life, love and the universe will become clearer. And your efforts will all seem infinitely more worthwhile. Like the poet William Blake, you will see and feel things that change your perception.

> To see a World in a Grain of Sand,
>   And a Heaven in a wild flower,
> Hold Infinity in the palm of your hand,
>   And Eternity in an hour.

Auguries of Innocence

Tomorrow is the first day of the rest of your life. Become an inner walker. Play around with inner walking – let it play around with you – and see where it takes you. And remember, you are your own best friend.